TEN KEYS to FREEDOM

Joy Linn

ISBN 978-1-64028-928-4 (paperback)
ISBN 978-1-64028-929-1 (digital)

Copyright © 2017 by Joy Linn

All rights reserved. No part of this publication may be reproduced, distributed, or transmitted in any form or by any means, including photocopying, recording, or other electronic or mechanical methods without the prior written permission of the publisher. For permission requests, solicit the publisher via the address below.

Christian Faith Publishing, Inc.
832 Park Avenue
Meadville, PA 16335
www.christianfaithpublishing.com

Printed in the United States of America

CONTENTS

Word from the Author 5
Acknowledgments 7

The First Key	Claim Your Redemption Rights	9
The Second Key	Step into the Blessings of God	19
The Third Key	Discover the Power of Your Words	31
The Fourth Key	Deal in Love	43
The Fifth Key	Forgive, Forgive, Forgive	53
The Sixth Key	Freedom from Fear	65
The Seventh Key	Claim God's Protection	77
The Eighth Key	Clearing Up Myths, Misconceptions, and Misinformation	87
The Ninth Key	Don't Deny the Power	111
The Tenth Key	Develop a Close Relationship with the Lord	125

WORD FROM THE AUTHOR

Before we begin our journey together through the *Ten Keys to Freedom*, please take a moment to read this letter. It will set the pace and the mood for what is to follow.

In Luke 8:5–15, Jesus gives us the parable of the sower, and then when his disciples asked him to explain the parable, He goes on to do so.

Basically, Jesus says that the "seed" in his parable is the Word of God. When it is planted in unbelieving hearts, those individuals allow Satan to steal it because their ground (their hearts or spirits) are unreceptive. The seed that fell on rocky ground refers to those whose hearts were not prepared for the seed; having shallow minds, they initially accept the Word, but when adversity of any kind comes along, they fall away from what they have heard. The seed that fell among thorns refers to those who allow the cares of this world and a preference for the things of the world's kingdom to choke the Word and it is unfruitful in them. The good ground refers to those with open and receptive hearts who are sincerely seeking to know the truth because only the truth can set them free. They are ready for the truth of God's Word and so they receive it; it sends its roots deep into their spirit and as a result it will grow and expand and "produce fruit."

Then in verse 18, Jesus says something that until recently, I didn't really understand. He says, "Take heed therefore how you hear for whosoever has, to him shall be given and whosoever has not, from him shall be taken even that which he seems to have."

I was looking at this from a material standpoint, and it made no sense that anyone having a lot of "things" would get more "things" and the person who had only a few "things" would have even them taken away. I prayed about this and asked the Lord to reveal to me the real meaning of this verse. After a time of meditating on the scripture, the Lord suggested I look at the Amplified Bible. I did so and was immediately able to see where I had missed it. The Amplified Bible sets it out this way, "Be careful therefore 'how' you listen. For to him who has (spiritual knowledge) will be given; and from him who does not have (spiritual knowledge), even what he thinks and guesses and supposes that he has will be taken away."

Jesus was not speaking of material things; He was speaking about "spiritual knowledge." The spiritual knowledge and understanding that comes from having open receptive ears and an open and receptive mind. The person who receives the seed of the Word and then takes it into their spirit, where it subsequently takes root and grows and expands, will increase their knowledge of the Word until their understanding is great in the things of God. To this person, as they grow in the Word, more will be unfolded to them. However, when a person goes by what they "think" and "guess" and "suppose" that they know and closes their spiritual ears to the truth of the Word of God, that person will eventually lose even what little they may have in the way of spiritual understanding. When that happens, they are vulnerable to the suggestions of Satan, and he will be quick to try and convince them the Word doesn't work.

I am asking you to be like the final example in Jesus' parable of the sower. Listen with open receptive ears and an open mind. Leave all preconceived ideas at the door and come to the table of God's Word with a willing heart hungry for answers only found in the precious Word of God

Let's begin!

ACKNOWLEDGMENTS

This book would not have been possible without the help and support of the special people in my life. To express how much I love and thank each one and how great has been their influence would require that I write another book.

THANK YOU FROM MY HEART!

To my sister "Nita" Anderson, you are a very special lady; I could write a volume and still not say it all. You've seen me through so much and been a loyal supporter of all my efforts.

To my dad, Herb Shuttleworth, without you, it just wouldn't have happened.

To my sister Lori Henderson, for being there for me when you were needed.

To my sister Kim Caylor, I'm so glad you're in my life.

To Mary Lou and Roger Morton, you have helped more than you know.

AND A VERY SPECIAL THANK YOU!

To my dear friend and editor, Louis Franks.

During his last illness, Louie was so determined to finish the editing of this book and to meet his personal commitment to me that until the day he went to be with the Lord, he worked diligently to accomplish all he'd pledged to do. I will be forever grateful for his dedication and his friendship.

We miss you, Louie!

REDEEMED

I've accepted Jesus Christ as Lord and Savior of my life;
I've been "redeemed"
I've taken a momentous step; I've been "born again," but
What does it really mean?

My sins have been forgiven and old things are passed away;
All things are brand new.
Jesus paid the price for me, it takes me to my knees,
And it should do the same for you!

But what has really happened; I really need to know;
What have I been given?
As wonderful as forgiveness is, could there be more to this
Than knowing when I die I go to Heaven?

What about the problems I face right here on earth?
How do I deal with sin?
How do I face the challenges that lie ahead?
Can I fight the good fight and win?

Are there answers to my questions; I know there must be;
How do I walk the narrow path I'm on?
I've been redeemed; and that is wonderful I know;
But I want to sing redemption's song!

In seeking for the answers that I really need to find;
Here is what, in my heart, I've heard:
I'm only going to find the answers in one place
In God's precious Word!

Let the journey begin!

THE FIRST KEY

Claim Your Redemption Rights

In order to put a claim on anything, you have to first understand the nature of what you are claiming. If, for example, you go on a trip and check your baggage through to your destination, they will give you a baggage claim ticket; at the end of your journey, you have something to prove that the bags in question are yours and you know of a certainty just what they look like. With your knowledge of what you are claiming and your proof of the right to claim it in hand you go to the kiosk indicated by the airlines and claim your baggage without a qualm. You have no question in your mind as to whether you have the right to claim your property and you have the proof of that right to show anyone who challenges you.

We should have at least that much confidence when making a claim on our redemptive rights in Christ. In this all-important first chapter of *Ten Keys to Freedom*, it is my hope and desire to show you what your *"redemption package"* consists of and to give you the *"claim ticket"* by which you can prove that it is yours. First, you will need to prove it to yourself and then you can share that proof with others, because if they are a child of God, it is theirs also.

A great majority of Christians today when they consider "redemption," think of redemption from sin; that is certainly a part of the package, but it is a long ways from the totality of your rights and privileges as a born-again child of God.

Before moving on to delineate just what your total redemption package consists of, let me take a moment to share with you the miraculous change that took place in you when you accepted Jesus Christ into your heart and your life. This step that you took in faith gave you more than just forgiveness of sins; the very life of God permeated your spirit and you became an entirely new you on the inside. It is just as the Word of God says, "Old things are passed away and behold all things are become new" (2 Cor. 5:17). I assume that you really know this; are you truly aware, however, of the vastness of what that implies? You have the very nature of God in your spirit! You have the *life* of God, you have the *love* of God, you have the *wisdom* of God, you have the *light* of God, *everything that God is now dwells in you!* If you will give place to the Spirit of God that indwells your spirit, He will teach you, guide you into all truth, and expand your understanding of the Word of God. The greater your grasp of God's Word, the greater the positive impact it will have on every area of your life. It is your door to freedom.

One of the most dramatic examples of what I am talking about came out of a wonderful book entitled *How You Can Be Led by the Spirit of God,* written by Dr. Kenneth E. Hagin. He tells the story of a woman we will call "Mary" who was so retarded from birth that she spent seven years in first grade and never even learned to write her name. Her teachers finally asked her parents to take her out of school. Her mother always brought her to church; however, her hair was always uncombed, her clothes were a sight, she crawled on the floor like a baby, stepped over pews to reach the one her mother was in, and she was an embarrassment to everyone around her. Then one night during an evangelistic meeting "Mary" came to the altar. There she accepted Christ and received eternal life—the Nature of God into her spirit. It was like a miracle when the very next night "Mary" came to church with her hair combed, her clothes neat and tidy, and her mentality seemed to have increased overnight.

Years later, Dr. Hagin went back to that church for a special service, and he asked the church secretary whatever happened to "Mary." She led him out to the porch and pointed to a housing development across from the church. She told him that Mary was building it, that she was a widow now, handled all her own money, was her own financier, and had three lovely children that were on the front pew every Sunday. She added that as church secretary, she could confirm that Mary's tithes and offerings were there every Sunday.

The Life of God came into her!

Never think that you were "just forgiven of sin" when you experienced the rebirth of your spirit. I wonder if we've even begun to know what we have received—the acquired vastness of our potential as a result of this most marvelous and miraculous experience. You became a brand-new person, more than a conqueror in Christ, filled with the very life essence of your limitless Heavenly Father.

Let's move on now and delve into the rest of your *redemption package*.

The more you look into just what is included, just how great the gift that was purchased for us at Calvary is, just how wide and how high and how deep is the subject of redemption, the more excited and thrilled and deeply grateful you will become. It will clarify for you many questions you may have had about your relationship with your Heavenly Father and your kinship with Jesus Christ as your Lord, Savior, and joint heir.

It will define the goodness of God for you and bring you to the realization that He only wants your very best and that He has, through the redemptive work of His Son on the cross, made available to you a whole new world of joy and love and peace, of freedom not only from sin but also from sickness and poverty and turmoil. The statement in John 3:16 that tells us "God so loved the world that He gave His only begotten Son that whosoever believes on Him shall have ever lasting life" will take on a whole new meaning. As you move forward to claim what has been made available to you, it will change your life, it will open up new avenues of understanding, it will free you in a way that you must experience to understand.

Understanding your redemption rights is the very foundation of every other key to freedom that is dealt with in this book. It is, if you will, the "Master Key" and the door that it opens will take you to a new way of life, a life so good, so rich in blessing that you will never consider going back to what life was like before you started down this pathway to freedom.

THE FIRST KEY

At this point, I'm fairly sure you are saying, "Okay, Joy, so what in the world is this wonderful "Master Key" you are raving about?"

I'm glad you asked. In order to answer your question, we are going to have to take a trip together; a trip back in time. No, this is not a science fiction book; this trip back in time will use the Word of God as its "time portal."

We have to go back to where it all began.

We have to go back to Genesis.

In chapter 1 of Genesis, starting with verse 26, "God said, Let us make man in our image, after our likeness and let them have dominion . . ." God later confers upon them dominion over all things on the earth. Dominion according to Webster encompasses "the power to rule, sovereign authority."

Then it says in verse 28, "And God blessed them." The words, "Be blessed; be fruitful and multiply and replenish the earth and subdue it!" are no doubt the first words that man heard.

Adam and Eve had it all: they had the Garden of Eden, they had a vast selection of food to choose from, and they were privileged to walk and talk with God in a face to face relationship. Genesis tells us that they fellowshipped together at the close of the day. They had total dominion, total authority over the earth and over everything that walked upon the earth, including the animals that were their friends at that point. They could partake of anything the Garden of Eden had to offer—with the exception of one tree the fruit of which was not to be eaten.

With all this going for them, they took an action that would not only affect them for the rest of their lives, but it would change the future for every living person that would evolve from them. They listened to the lies and deception of Satan and took of the fruit that was forbidden.

With this one act of disobedience, Adam and Eve turned their God-given authority over to Satan, and he became the illegitimate ruler of this earth. Adam had the right to transfer his authority and that is exactly what he did. As a result of Satan's illegal takeover, the earth became cursed, and Satan became the God of it. It was a downward spiral of disaster from there. His authority cut a path of destruction throughout the era of the Old Testament. Only by staying within the protection of God by keeping His commandments did God's people escape the ravages of the curse.

A dear friend once told me that she was literally raised on a church bench, but until fairly recently, she had never known that Satan was the God of this world (2 Corinthians 4:4, John 12:31, John 16:11, and Ephesians 6:12). It clarified a great deal for her to realize that it was Satan, not God, who caused disaster. We will cover what to do to prevent disaster in your life later in this book, but let me just say here that Satan can only hurt you with your permission. The reason I can say that is because what Adam gave away (his authority over all the earth) Jesus got back and He gave it to us. We will talk more about that later.

Regardless of the fact that Adam's disobedience brought about grave consequences for him and all that would follow him, God never changes and what He gives He does not take back. God's covenant with Adam was a *blessing covenant* and God does not break His covenant Word. Adam and Eve paid a high price for their actions, but the blessing of God was still on them and their descendants.

Let's fast forward to Noah who came out of the genealogic line of Adam's son, Seth. The line ended with Methuselah whose son, Lamech, was Noah's father. If you remember the story from Sunday school days, Noah found favor with God and was saved (he and his family) from the destruction of the flood. After the waters receded, Noah came out of the ark and built an altar to the Lord. In Genesis chapter 9 verse 1, it says, "God blessed Noah and his sons and said to them, be fruitful, and multiply and replenish the earth."

Sound familiar? It should because it is almost the exact words said to Adam. And so God's blessing was declared once again and bestowed on Noah and his prodigy. One thing changed. Satan got to Adam and Eve by using a serpent. After the flood, God put the fear of mankind upon the animals so that they could never be used again in that manner. God's covenant of blessing, however, stayed the same.

Now let's fast forward once more to a man named *Abram*, who came from the direct line of Shem. Shem was Noah's son and the most dedicated to God of Noah's offspring. In Abram, God found a man who would recognize who He was and would put his faith in Him. He called him out from his home and his people because they were idol worshippers, and it was necessary to remove him from that influence.

Abram was seventy-five years old when he left all that he had ever known and struck out in faith alone to go where God would lead him. God eventually renamed him. Abram became Abraham (meaning a "father of many nations") and his wife Sarai became Sarah, which means "princess" and God said he would make her a mother of nations.

In Gen. 12:2 and 3, after telling him to leave his home and go where God would lead him, God said to him, "I will make you a great nation, and I will bless you and make your name great; and you shall be a blessing," and later in that verse, "in you shall all families of the earth be blessed."

I will bless you so you can be a blessing. And so the blessing of God was stated once again, and this time, it was extended not only to Abraham but to "all the families of the earth." God kept His Word and richly blessed Abraham. Genesis 13:2 tells us that he "was very rich in cattle, in silver and in gold."

Abraham was not perfect, but although he made mistakes along the way, he never lost sight of who God was—"the most high God, possessor of heaven and earth," and as the Word says, "He believed God; and it was counted to him for righteousness." Abraham was faithful; he tithed to Melchizedek, the High Priest of God, and walked according to God's precepts. But because the promised blessing was so great and far-reaching, in the fifteenth chapter of Genesis, Abraham asks for proof that he was to inherit this blessing. God's response was to enter into one of the strongest covenants ever recorded between God and a man until Jesus cut the new covenant in His own blood. God made a covenant with Abraham in the blood of animals, and because Abraham understood the power and implications of a blood covenant, he was satisfied that the blessing was to him, his prodigy, and eventually would be extended to all the families of the earth.

Many people today do not comprehend the true meaning of a blood covenant. If your ethnic background is American Indian, you would completely comprehend just what it means to enter into a blood covenant with someone. It constitutes a pledge to stand with each other through thick and thin—to do whatever it might take to protect, honor, stand by, and support each other even if it requires giving up your life to do so. In this commitment between God and the man Abraham God, who could swear by no greater, swore by Himself (Heb. 6:13) cutting the covenant in the blood of animals. It was so powerful that God knew Satan would challenge its validity. Later in Abraham's life, God would ask him to sacrifice Isaac, his son of promise; Abraham goes so far as raising his knife to take the life of his only son, but an angel stays his hand. God said He would count it as done, and so Abraham was proven willing and able to meet the terms of his covenant with God. Their contract had, in effect, been ratified. All of heaven must have held their breath during this experience. You see, because Abraham was willing to give *his* son, God could now put into motion the events that would lead to the giving of *His* son as a sacrifice for us all. Gives you a whole new slant on the story, doesn't it?

Abraham's son Isaac grew up under the influence of his father's faith. In Genesis chapter 26, God appeared to Isaac and once again reiterated the blessing. He says in verse 3, *"I will be with you and will bless you; for to you and your seed I will give all these countries and I will perform the oath which I swore to Abraham your father."* In verse 4 God once again declares that *"in your seed shall all the nations of the earth be blessed."* God kept His Word and everything that Isaac touched was blessed. God always keeps His Word!

God restates his promised covenant blessing to *Jacob*, Isaac's son in Gen. 28:13 and 14, telling him basically the same thing—that through him and his seed, all the families of the earth would be blessed.

That blessing was evident in Jacob's son, *Joseph*, who was sold into slavery by his brothers, only to end up ruler over all the land of Egypt under Pharaoh because God was with him and blessed him. As a result, Joseph was able to save the nations from starvation. This was a great example of a man being blessed so that he could be a blessing.

After God's covenant promise was cut in blood with Abraham, it was declared again and again. Eventually, *God called Moses*, a Hebrew man raised by an Egyptian princess, to rescue the children of Israel

THE FIRST KEY

from the oppression of the Egyptians. Over the course of time, God gave Moses the law in order to explain the nature of sin to a people who needed to have it delineated.

In Deuteronomy 28:1–14, the blessings of Abraham were finally defined. Basically, those blessing include freedom from sin, sickness, poverty, mental turmoil, and protection from all harm. The balance of that chapter sets out the curses. They are listed in great detail, however, to simplify what is covered in Deuteronomy 28—*if it is good it's the blessing; if it's bad it's the curse.*

God never changes; as James 1:17 says, "Every good gift and every perfect gift is from above and comes down from the Father of lights, with whom (there) is no variableness, neither shadow of turning." God made a blood covenant with Abraham to bless him and make him a blessing and that blessing echoes down through the Old Testament.

You might say, "Yes, but that was the Old Testament."

Well, *fasten your seat belt and turn to Galatians 3:13 and 14.* It says, "Christ has redeemed us from the curse of the law, being made a curse for us; for it is written, cursed is every one that hangs on a tree (so) that *the blessing of Abraham might come on the Gentiles* through Jesus Christ; that we might receive the promise of the Spirit through faith."

If you can't grasp the impact of that, your wood is wet!

Your redemption package includes all the blessings of Abraham; there is one proviso, one initial and necessary step that you must take to claim what is yours.

Obtaining the blessing of Abraham for us is a gift dearly bought and paid for by our precious Lord. When you receive a gift, two things are involved. First, *you must accept it*, and secondly, *you must use it* in order to make it your own. You certainly would not beg and plead with the giver to give you what is already yours to take, use, and enjoy. You would accept the gift and thank the giver. Then you would unwrap the package and incorporate its contents into the pattern of your life.

So that's it. The redemption package is yours; you have the biblical "claim ticket" to prove that it is yours, but you must accept it.

Once you have accepted that the blessings of Abraham are yours for the taking, then you must study to renew your mind to the Word of God and find out what steps you will need to take in order to bring into full manifestation what God has in store for you.

Your Covenant with God

From the moment your spirit was reborn, God entered into a covenant relationship with you. A covenant is simply a binding agreement between two parties. There are stipulations on both sides of the agreement (i.e., I will agree to do this if you will agree to do that).

Part of reaping the benefits of your covenant with God involves doing what God in His Word asks you to do. Jesus said, "My yoke is easy and my burden is light" (Matt. 11:30) and according to Third John 2, God wishes above all things that you prosper and be in health. With this in mind, it would behoove you to determine what guide lines God has set out for you to follow.

The *next nine keys to freedom* will cover what those guidelines are and what steps you need to take in order for you to inherit the blessings that are yours as a child of God. *His requirements are not only needed for you to inherit the blessings but they will be, in themselves, a source of blessing to you.*

Following God's blueprint for your life will take you to a new level of spiritual growth that will positively impact your circumstances . . .

The benefits of living in accordance with God's guidelines are these:

> Peace
>> Joy
>>> Health
>>>> Prosperity
>>>>> Protection
>>>>>> A closer walk with your
>>>>>> Heavenly Father.

Now that's a deal you can't refuse.
Read on . . .

BLESSED

I'm blessed! I'm blessed! What a great discovery!
What great news—I've been redeemed!
Not just from sin but from sickness and poverty!
I'm beginning to see just what redemption means.

It may take a little time to put old ideas aside.
And open up my mind to what seems brand new.
I'll need to put away all prejudice and pride;
But I'll rely on God's Word and you should too!

What God's Word says I'm redeemed from
I'll accept within my heart.
I'll trust God's promises are true.
I'll let the blessings start!

THE SECOND KEY

Step into the Blessings of God

In our last chapter, we traced the history of God's blessing back to the first covenant of blessing God entered into which was with Adam. This **blessing covenant** was then reaffirmed with Noah—established in blood with Abraham; reaffirmed with Isaac, Jacob, and Joseph; and finally clearly defined through Moses in the twenty-eighth chapter of Deuteronomy.

Before proceeding with the steps needed in order to take advantage of all that Jesus made available to anyone who becomes a child of God, I want to say a word about Deuteronomy 28. What I am about to share with you is true not only in Deuteronomy but throughout the Old Testament. If you decided to read Deuteronomy 28 through for yourself to see what the *blessings* are and what the *curses* are, then you may have wondered about one thing, and I want to help clear up an issue that may have bothered you. I know it bothered me for a long time until my research revealed what I am about to tell you.

God is in the blessing business; He is not in the cursing business. Yet as you read Deuteronomy 28, it looks like God not only caused the children of Israel to be "blessed" but to be "cursed" if they did not obey His commandments. I discovered that in the Hebrew language the verb form is either "*permissive*" or "*causative*." The King James translators used the "causative" verb form. When God's people during that era did not follow His precepts and keep His commandments, they placed themselves out of the wall of His protection, thus making them subject to the curses. God is the author of blessing; Satan is the author of the curse.

In Deuteronomy 28:22 for instance, the King James Version of the Bible says, "The Lord will smite thee with consumption," but in the original Hebrew, that same phrase really says, "The Lord shall allow you to be smitten." The diseases were there because of the curse; God did not cause the sicknesses that are described; He *did* allow them. Let me explain why.

Adam sinned and turned his God-given authority over to Satan. Adam became subservient to him and Satan became the illegitimate ruler of this world. From that point on, the very earth became cursed. The only protection that people had was the protection provided by Almighty God. However, the wages of sin are death, and if the people of God in the days covered by the Old Testament did not walk in accordance with God's will for them and walked in sin instead, they removed themselves from the wall of God's protection and became subject to the curse that Satan brought to the earth.

This, in effect, tied God's hands. As long as Satan had authority on earth, God had to allow the curses to come on those living outside of His protection. Authority on earth had been given to man; man transferred it to Satan, and although God certainly had the power to override that transaction, He could not do so because it would have been breaking His word and breaching His covenant with Adam.

God does not "*cause*" the disasters that come into our lives; He is not the author of sickness and gets no glory or pleasure from it. *He gets honor and glory and pleasure from seeing you well.* God will take any bad situation you get yourself into and turn it around for your good, but that is not the same thing as causing it.

With the new covenant, the authority issue has been dealt with.

If a child has been kidnapped, the parents wait for the kidnapper to call and set the amount of the ransom. They will gladly pay it to redeem their child. In this analogy, you and I are the "children" kidnapped by Satan and Jesus, the unblemished Lamb of God was the ransom paid for our redemption.

After his sacrificial death, Jesus took the keys of hell and death from Satan; made a show of him openly (Col. 2:15, Eph. 4:9, Rev.

1:18) and recaptured the authority given to Satan by Adam and then ***Jesus gave that authority back to us*** (Matt. 28:18–20; Mark 16:17, 18). Now Satan's hands are tied and all he can do is try to use any willing or ignorant man or woman to bring about his evil. If you stand against him in Jesus' name, he is out of the game and you win. That's what the scripture means when it says, "We are more than conquerors in Christ . . ." (Rom. 8:37).

Matthew. 16:19 says, "That which you bind on earth is bound in Heaven and that which you loose on earth is loosed in Heaven." The power to bind and loose is ours. We have the power and authority to prevent Satan's intervention in our lives.

Take God at His Word, take your God-given authority, and bind Satan and all of his cohorts in Jesus' name. Stand up on your spiritual hind legs, flex your spiritual muscle, and say, "In the name of the Lord Jesus Christ I bind the principalities and powers and rulers of darkness of this world; I bind and put down spiritual wickedness in high places and render them harmless and ineffective against me and my loved ones; and I loose the power of the living God into each and every one of my circumstances." Base your words on God's Word in Matt. 28:19 and Eph. 6:12.

Seeing the Blessing Manifest for You

Having established that you have the authority to control your circumstances, *let's find the key that will open the door* to all of God's blessings so that you can begin to see them manifest in your life.

We have defined the nature and intent of God's blessing and based upon the fact that God cannot lie and never goes back on His Word; we have determined that the blessings of Abraham belong to every born again child of God.

Why then are so many Christians poor, downtrodden, sick, and in turmoil?

Why indeed!

We might also ask, "Since salvation is a free gift which has been dearly bought and paid for why are there so many unsaved people in the world today?" The answer is simple; either because they don't know about it, or they do know about it but have not chosen to accept the gift.

A great many Christians simply have not been told about the *blessings of God* and are completely in the dark regarding the fact that God wants to bless them. *What you don't know about you can't take advantage of* and many Christians know nothing about their redemptive rights in Christ. The Word says, "My people perish for lack of knowledge" (Hos. 4:6).

Don't let Satan rob you of the blessings gained through our Lord Jesus because of lack of knowledge.

Don't let Satan rob you of the blessings of God that are rightfully yours because of what your grandma or your Great-Aunt Tilley **said** was in the Bible—go to the book and find out firsthand what God has provided for you in His Word.

Gifts are gifts; we do not earn them—they are freely given. Your salvation was free and involved only your acceptance. The gift of God's redemption from sickness, poverty, and turmoil also requires acceptance. Once you accept salvation and your spirit is reborn, you are now eligible for all the other benefits that come from your new status. Finding out about these benefits and having them start to operate in your life will require that you *do the research*; get into the Word, study it, immerse yourself in it, keep it before your eyes and in your ears, and when your heart is filled with the truth of God's Word, it will start to come out of your mouth. Commit to this and you will start to believe what you are reading and subsequently saying. When you reach that point, faith will result. "Faith comes by hearing and hearing by the Word of God" (Rom. 10:17). Faith is acting on what you believe and as you do so, everything that you believe will start to manifest in your life.

The Role of Faith

You were saved by faith (Eph. 2:8); you live by faith (Rom. 1:17); faith without works is dead (James 2:17); without faith it is impossible to please God (Heb. 11:6); through faith (with patience) we inherit the promises (Heb. 6:12); faith overcomes the world

(1 John 5:4); we walk by faith not by sight (2 Cor. 5:7); faith is the substance of things hoped for and the evidence of things not seen (with the five physical senses) (Heb. 11:1) and the list goes on.

It is obvious that faith is the key to partaking of the many blessings God has provided for you. Finding the faith to believe God's Word is true will bring you to a point where you believe without any doubt that what is said in the Word of God is for you; that it is the path you need to walk on, and that *whatever He says is yours to claim, is yours to claim*. At that point, you will speak out in faith and claim every advantage of your redemptive rights in Christ Jesus!

One more word about faith—it works by love (Gal. 5:6), and it is under girded by patience. Faith and patience are called the power twins. When you *believe* the Word, you believe God because God and His Word are one; faith will be the result and you will enter the process of believing and receiving.

The Process of Believing and Receiving

This process of believing and receiving is neither difficult nor hard to understand.

First you need to firmly **believe** that God wants to bless you.

Second you need to **live by the guidelines** set out in God's Word.

Third you need to **start claiming the blessings** in faith.

Let's talk about believing:

Believe God wants to bless you!

In order to reach a point of faith in God's desire to bless you in every area of your life, you will need to delve into His Word. The more you concentrate on anything, the bigger it gets within you. That is true, regardless of what you are focusing on. If you focus on the seeming impossibility of a situation, it will overwhelm you. If you focus on the answer to the problem, the problem will diminish. If you are in the dark, you need to concentrate on any glimmer of light.

As you concentrate on God's Word, it will get more and more real to you; you will fill your heart with its truth, and before long, it will start to come out of your mouth. You will speak the truth of God's Word into every circumstance and you will begin to see those circumstances change for the better. This will lead you to **believe** that *anything God's Word says you are, you are; anything God's Word says you can do, you can do and whatever dream God has put in your heart He will make a way for it to become a reality.*

There is great power in believing. Believing and receiving is emphasized all throughout the New Testament. Mark 11:23 and 24 gives us a clear picture of the process. This is Jesus speaking, "For verily I say unto you that whosoever shall say unto this mountain, 'Be thou removed and be thou cast into the sea;' and shall not doubt in his heart, but shall **believe** that those things which he says shall come to pass; he shall have whatsoever he says . . . What things so ever you desire, when you pray **believe** that you receive them and you shall have them." Then in Matt. 21:22 Jesus says, "And all things, whatsoever you shall ask in prayer, **believing**, you shall receive."

These passages of scripture are confirmation of the fact that speaking God's Word and believing God's Word will move the mountains in our life; and it further confirms that prayer requests made in faith will be answered.

The Placebo Effect

I read an article recently regarding the power of believing. It told of a newsletter from the Mayo Health Clinic which described what they called the "placebo effect." A placebo, as you know, contains no active medication, but is used on patients who **believe** they are being treated with real medicine.

In a series of experiments, doctors filled capsules with sugar or flour and prescribed them to patients who were told that they were receiving potent medicine. The patients **believed** the pills would make them well; many of them started improving almost immediately. This *placebo effect* has been used to treat numerous diseases. Some of the recipients of the placebos even reported side effects of the drug they *believed* they were receiving and in some cases their use had to be terminated gradually to prevent withdrawal symptoms. All of these responses to placebos occurred because patients *believed* they had received something that would make them well.

If the power of believing can be so obviously evidenced in a scientific experiment such as the one described in this article; think how much more powerful believing is when connected to the Word of God!

Check Out Your Benefits

Find out what the Word says about *healing*, about your *finances*, about God's willingness to bless you, or about any other issue that you may face in life.

Renew your mind with the Word of God, get it into your heart (spirit) in abundance by speaking it over every situation in life, and you will reach a place where you unequivocally believe what God is saying. This makes for such strong faith that nothing will seem impossible to you because all things are possible with God and you are the channel through which He will accomplish all the dreams He has put in your heart.

The next step you will need to take will come with time as you grow deeper and deeper in the knowledge of God and the realization that *He loves you and wants to bless you*. The divine wisdom that comes with spending time in God's Word will bring you to a place where you will determine to always live within God's guidelines.

Living Within God's Guidelines!

For example, the Word says "love is the last commandment" so you will need to *deal in love*. The Word says "forgive not seven times but seventy times seven" so *forgiveness will need to become a way of life* for you. The Word says, "seek first the Kingdom of Heaven and all these things shall be added to you" this means *you will need to put God first in your life* and determine to develop a deeper relationship with the Lord.

THE SECOND KEY

Please remember there is a reason for everything that we are told to abide by, and every guideline is for our highest good. Later in this book, there is a chapter on dealing in love, which sets out the need to live this way and gives you all the reasons this will bless you including the fact that faith works by love (Gal. 5:6). There is also a later chapter on forgiving with all the good it can bring into your life. The last chapter of this book covers the need to develop a closer relationship with Jesus and delineates the blessed results of doing so.

Claiming the Blessing!

You've built your faith, you've reached a place where you believe the Word of God, you've determined to walk in God's precepts, now you need to take the next step. Start claiming the blessings. *Be bold!* We are told to come boldly before the throne of grace that we might receive. So be bold and *claim what is rightfully yours as a child of God.*

Let me add one word here regarding asking God for something and ending your prayer with "if it be Thy will." When you are seeking God regarding direction for your life such as a call to the ministry or something God is dealing with you about that applies only to you, then asking for His will in the situation is applicable. Afterward, you will want to learn to listen to your inner witness and let God guide you in the direction He would have you go. If, however, you are approaching the Throne of Grace and asking for something that is clearly set out in God's Word, you **know** His will because you have His Word on it. God's Word *is* His will. Once you have determined that your claim is in accordance with the Word of God, you can proceed with confidence to make your request.

Here are some examples of making a claim in accordance with your Word backed rights and privileges:

For Healing

"Thank you, Lord for my healing; I claim it in Jesus name. Your Word says "by His stripes I was healed" and if I was, I am and so I claim healing from the top of my head to the bottom of my feet" (1 Peter 2:24).

"Christ has redeemed me from the curse of the law, therefore I forbid any sickness or disease to come on this body; any germ or virus that touches this body dies instantly in Jesus name. Every cell, every tissue, every organ of this body functions in the perfection to which God created it to function and there shall be no malfunction in this body in Jesus name" (Gal. 3:13, Rom. 8:11, Gen. 1:31 and Matt. 16:19).

For Needs to be Met

"Father, Your Word tells me that as I give it shall be given unto me, good measure, pressed down, running over men will give unto my bosom; (Luke 6:38) therefore I claim that all my needs are met and as I gladly give of my tithe I can expect and I hereby claim the windows of Heaven blessing" (Mal. 3:10).

Dealing with the Opposition

You will need to stand against Satan's efforts to get to your mind and thus get you off tract. Stand on the Word that tells you that if you *"resist the devil he will flee from you"* (James 4:7). Tell him in Jesus' name to take his hands off God's property—you." The word "flee" in the scripture I've quoted here, in the Greek means "flee as if in terror." This gives you a whole new concept of Satan; he's a defeated foe; Jesus whipped him soundly and he trembles at the name of Jesus, so use it as a weapon against anything he tries to throw at you and he'll back off every time.

Am I Declaring a Lie?

At this point you may ask, "How can I declare that all my needs are met when I don't know how I'm going to pay my bills; isn't that a lie?" The answer is, *"No it is not a lie; you are simply declaring the truth of God's Word.* It is doing what God does." The Word says that God "calls those things that are not as though they were" (Rom. 4:17). We are supposed to do the same thing.

Standing in Faith

The Word says, "**Having done all, stand**" (Eph. 6:13). While you are standing in faith for the manifestation of the blessings of the Lord in your life, start praising and thanking God for the answer **even before it manifests!** The moment you claimed it, it was done in the Spirit, so call it done and thank God for it until it begins to evidence itself in your life.

Don't Back Up

Don't let Satan deceive you into thinking that just because the answers to your prayers haven't manifested they are not going to be answered. Satan is a liar! Jesus called him the "father of liars" (John 8:44). *Don't fall for his lies!* The Word says he comes to kill, steal, and destroy (John 10:10). *Don't let him steal your joy.* He is the great deceiver (Rev. 12:9). *Don't let him deceive you.* He is not an innovator, he never comes up with anything new, and all he can do is go about **like** a roaring lion seeking whom he can devour (1 Peter 5:8) Ignore his roar; he is **LIKE** a lion but his teeth were pulled a long time ago so don't give him any place in your life. *Don't let him discourage you*, and don't let him cause you to give up on what you have come to believe! We are told to "fight the good fight of faith" (1 Tim. 6:12) and to "put on the whole armor of God so that we can stand against the wiles of the devil" (Eph. 6:11). It's a **GOOD FIGHT** because you win if you will just hang in there. It is in this time of "standing in faith" that you could lose the battle; so just remember we are more than conquerors in Christ and that no weapon formed against you can prosper (Rom. 8:37, Isa. 54:17). In other words, *encourage yourself in what the Word of God says about you* and your rights and privileges in Christ. Keep thanking God for your answers. They ***WILL MANIFEST***!

Are You Ready to Receive?

Your Heavenly Father loves you and wants only the very best for you. His *covenant blessings* are yours. If you will believe and exercise your faith; you will receive.

I sincerely hope that at this point, you are ready to step into the blessings of God, that you have come to believe that these blessings are yours, bought and paid for by our Lord and Savior Jesus Christ, and that whatever changes you will need to make in your life, you are ready to make them. With that happy thought in mind, let me now give you all the keys you will need to revolutionize your life and affairs, to walk in victory under the protection of God Almighty and to know the joy and fulfillment that can only come by living in accordance with the specific guidelines set out by God in His Word.

You will soon know what Jesus meant when he said, "He whom the Son sets free is free indeed" (John 8:36).

Let the journey begin!

WORDS, WORDS, WORDS

God said, LIGHT BE!
And with His Word,
Light became a reality.
There is power in God's Word.

I was created in His image!
Yet I've never given it a thought.
I've never tried to gage
The power in my words and what they've wrought.

God's Word says that life and death
Are in the power of the tongue.
And I can't even begin to guess
What my words in the past have begun.

But today for me is a brand new day.
I repent of every idle word I've ever said.
And from now on I'll watch what I say.
I'll put the past behind and stride ahead.

I'll open up to all God has for me.
I'll guard my mouth and I will overcome!
I'll choose life; and the results that I will see;
Are positive circumstances and battles won!

THE THIRD KEY

Discover the Power of Your Words

The doors of truth that were opened to me when I began to realize the power of words altered the course of my life.

Charles Capps is a gifted minister whose books on the spoken word have always been a light to my path. I recently received a pamphlet on the subject of words by Rev. Capps entitled, "Words Establish or Change Circumstances," and that really says it all. Words are powerful. Words create or destroy. Words bring fulfillment or disaster. Words are a force for good or evil. The spoken word holds a dynamo of power that can change your world into one in which you have health, financial security, protection, and true happiness. Used negatively, however, the spoken word can be your undoing; can bring illness, poverty, unhappiness; and can open the door to the enemy of your soul.

James 3:10 says it well, "Out of the same mouth proceeds blessing and cursing. My brethren, these things ought not to be."

Imitate God as His Dear Children (Eph. 5:1)

In order to grasp what I have just said about the power of words for good or evil, you must see a picture of the nature of God. From Gen. 1:3 through Gen. 1:26, the words "And God said" are repeated eight times. Why the repetition? Wouldn't it have been easier to say, "God said" just once and then list all that He said? I believe that the repetition is to emphasize the fact that God SPOKE the world into existence. God SAID "Light be" and light was! God's Words have creative power that is almost unfathomable to the finite mind. The creative power of God's spoken Word is an intricate part of the very nature of God.

Now let's look at Gen. 1:27. "So God created man in his own image, in the image of God created he him, male and female created he them."

You were created in the image of God!

Jesus said to the Samaritan woman, "God is a Spirit and those that worship him must do so in spirit and in truth" (John 4:24).

You are a spirit, you live in a body and you have a soul which is your mind, will, and emotions.

God is love!

As a born-again child of the living God, you have His love within you.

God's Word reaches into the spiritual and manifests in the natural.

You have the same ability. By speaking the truth of God's Word, you bring spiritual truth into the natural world and, in effect, you create your own circumstances.

If your circumstances aren't too wonderful right now, start listening to the words of your mouth.

The Power of the Spoken Word

There is a vast amount of information regarding the spoken word in the Bible. From Genesis to Revelation, you will find the admonition to guard your tongue and watch your words. We are under the authority of words from the moment we are born on this earth.

We are saved by hearing and speaking words.
We are filled with the Spirit by hearing and speaking words.

We build our faith by hearing words until they can be found in our hearts in abundance; at this point, these words are the ones that will come out of our mouth.

The words we hear as children can influence our entire lives.

James 3:1–7 tells us that if any man offend not in word, he is a perfect man (mature) and able to bridle his whole body. James goes on to give as an example the bit in a horse's mouth, which turns the entire horse and the helm (rudder) of a ship, which turns the whole ship. This is saying that we, in effect, are the captain of the ship of our lives and can steer the course of our future by the words we speak into our circumstances.

Proverbs 18:21 puts it clearly. It says, "Death and life are in the power of the tongue." The original Hebrew for the word interpreted "power" actually means "hand." That may seem strange but think about it for a moment. If you have a project for me and I agree to handle it; you would say to me, "Okay, Joy, I'm leaving the responsibility for the outcome of this project in your hands." So the Word of God is telling us that life and death are in the control (or hands) of the tongue and that we are responsible for the results of what comes out of our mouth.

The following are just a very few of the many scriptures that deal with the power of our words.

"Death and life are in the power of the tongue" (Prov. 18:21).

"He that guards his mouth keeps his life, but he that opens wide his lips comes to ruin" (Prov. 13:3, Amp).

"There are those who speak rashly, like the piercing of a sword, but the tongue of the wise brings healing" (Prov. 12:18, Amp).

"Thou art snared with the words of thy mouth" (Prov. 6:2).

"He who guards his mouth and his tongue keeps himself from troubles" (Prov. 21:23, Amp).

"They overcame by the blood of the Lamb, and by the word of their testimony" (Rev. 12:11).

As James said in the third chapter, if you control what you say, you can control your body and your entire nature.

Does what you say reflect in your circumstances? Yes, indeed.

What you constantly declare with your mouth will eventually manifest in your life. For example, if you declare the truth of the Word of God regarding health (by His stripes I am healed) (1 Peter 2:24 and Isa. 53:5); if you declare God's Word regarding finances (God supplies all my needs in accordance with His riches in glory) (Phil. 4:19); or (It is God who gives me power to get wealth) (Deut. 8:18). or (the blessing of the Lord it maketh rich and He adds no sorrow with it) (Prov. 10:22); if you declare God's Word regarding divine wisdom (the Spirit of Truth abides in me and teaches me all things) (John 16:13) or (I have the wisdom of God) (James 1:5); or if you declare the Word of God regarding any other issue of life, then you will live in the blessings of God that He intends for you to enjoy. You will take full advantage of your redemption rights.

If, on the other hand, you are constantly declaring the circumstances (I believe I'm catching the flu), bemoaning the situation (I never get any good breaks), or using negative words such as *death*, *sick*, *tired*, etc., as figures of speech (He scared me to death; I'm sick and tired of this): then you are sowing seeds that can only bring a negative harvest.

Choose Life!

The Word of God says in Deut. 30:19, "I set before you this day, life and death—choose life." Notice, you have a choice. You can choose to speak life and joy and blessing—health, peace, and prosperity into your world. Or you can choose to fail to put a guard on your lips and end up creating a very different set of circumstances. It is really up to you.

This may sound simple, but believe me, it really isn't. You will need all the help your Heavenly Father can give you. David in Psalms 141:3 prayed, "Set a watch, O Lord, before my mouth; keep the door of my lips." We need to pray the same prayer.

We should not be speaking cross wise of the Word of God by using negative words as figures of speech. Let me give you a few examples of what I am talking about:

THE DEATH WORD

"He scared me to death." "I laughed until I thought I'd die." "That dress in the window is to die for." "That child will be the death me." "My feet are killing me." These are just a few of the uses of the death word.

THE FEAR WORD

"I'm afraid I can't make our meeting." "He put the fear of God into me." "I'm afraid not." "I'm afraid I'm going to be late." "I'm afraid this isn't going to work." "These are just a few of the use of fear as a figure of speech." Any statement that starts out "I fear" or "I'm afraid" is negative usage.

THE UNBELIEF WORD

"I don't believe I need another helping." "I don't believe I understand what you are saying." "Seeing is believing." "I don't believe we are available on that date." "I can't believe he did that." These are all misuses of the word *believe*. Any statement that starts out "I don't believe" is negative usage. You are a believer and shouldn't be constantly declaring that you aren't.

THE TIRED AND SICK WORDS

"I'm sick and tired of this situation." "I'm really tired of this class." "I'm tired of the way so and so is acting." "I'm weary of the entire situation." "I'm sick and tired of waiting." These are a very few of the ways we use both of these words as figures of speech. "I'm sick and tired" is negative usage. You are strong in the Lord; the joy of the Lord is your strength and you should be affirming that on a daily basis.

THE THIRD KEY

THE SORRY WORD

We state "I'm sorry" constantly; as a child of God, you've been redeemed from sorrow. If you need to apologize just ask for forgiveness or say "excuse me I didn't mean to do or say that." Sorrow is part of the curse and we've been redeemed from the curse. Isa. 53:4 and 5 says, "Surely he has borne our *griefs* and carried our *sorrows*; yet we did esteem Him stricken, smitten of God and afflicted. But He was wounded for our transgressions, He was bruised for our iniquities; the chastisement of our peace was upon Him; and with His stripes we are healed." He carried our *griefs* and *sorrows* so that we don't have to just as surely as he took our sins upon Himself. He took our sins, assured us of healing by His stripes, bore our griefs and sorrows so that we can live life free from the guilt of sin and the curse of sickness and the weight of sorrow and depression. I sincerely believe Christians that fight depression may be bringing it into their lives by the constant use of the sorry word.

The Process Isn't Easy

When you begin the culling-out process to get rid of all the negative words you're using as figures of speech; you will understand what I mean when I say it isn't easy. You will need God's help and a great deal of determination. The rewards, however, are well worth the effort.

When I first discovered the truth regarding the power of my words I determined to change my ways and start declaring the truth of God's Word. I also asked God to help me eliminate any negative words from my vocabulary. I thought that part would be a snap, but I was wrong. I became almost speechless for a long time because I had used some of the "death," "tired," "sick," and "worry" words as figures of speech for so long that I was really unaware of how much I was using them. For instance, I used the phrase "to die for" regarding the possession of something wonderful (isn't that irony). Anyway, I had to change that to "to live for," which sounded strange to me at first. After a while, however, "to die for" sounded awkward to my ears and "to live for" seemed a comfortable expression. In time, I managed to cull out all the negative culprits that had insinuated themselves into my speech patterns. It didn't happen overnight. I did find, however, that the best way to remove old patterns of speech was to create new ones. My mother who was a Christian psychologist used to admonish me to get rid of bad habit patterns by creating new ones that were good habits patterns. This works with any mental groove that you have established by continual use. The key to changing any negative mental groove is to create a new and positive one. Mother was a very wise woman. I used her advice and little by little replaced the negative usage with positive usage and began to speak the truth of the Word of God into my circumstances. I came to realize that as I filled my heart with the Word of God and it got into my spirit it became easier and easier to declare the spiritual reality regarding whatever circumstances I faced (the mountains in my life).

In a very real way, taming your tongue and determining with God's help to speak only the truth of God's Word is a major key to your personal and financial freedom.

As I've mentioned previously, I've been asked if declaring, "All my needs are met according to God's riches in glory" isn't really lying when I'm in financial crisis and don't know how I'm going to get through the month? Let me once again give you the answer to that question.

No, it isn't! Declaring the reality of what God has promised in His Word is pure truth. You are following your Heavenly Father's example of "calling those things which be not as though they were" (Rom. 4:17). The only way you are going to eventually change your circumstances is to keep declaring the spiritual truth until it builds your faith for what you have need of and brings it into manifestation.

This is true regarding anything you are standing in faith for—healing, financial breakthrough, the salvation of a loved one, wisdom to deal with the challenges in your life or any mountain of adversity that you face and need to remove.

Keep Sowing Your Seed

In regard to financial blessing, keep sowing your seed by tithing on what you have, and even if it is a very small amount, be faithful, keep declaring God's Word on the subject and you will see a good harvest if you stand in faith and faint not! Fighting the good fight of faith is what God's Word calls this procedure. It is a fight, but as I've said before, the reason it's a "good fight" is if you will hang in there, you will win.

The Word of Jesus on it.

One truth that is absolutely essential if you are going to succeed in the area of speaking the positive truth of God's Word can be found in Matt. 12:34. Jesus is speaking, "For out of the abundance of the heart the mouth speaks. A good man out of the good treasure of the heart brings forth good things; and an evil man out of the evil treasure brings forth evil things." Then in verse 37, He adds, "For by your words you shall be justified, and by your words you shall be condemned." This scripture makes it clear beyond any doubt that whatever you have in abundance in your heart is what comes out of your mouth. You need to plant the truth of God's Word in your heart! How do you do that? By getting into His Word daily, absorbing its truths, listening to CDs that rightly divide the Word of truth, exposing yourself to God's Word until it begins to generate faith in you. In Rom. 10:17, it says, "Faith comes by hearing and hearing by the Word of God." Once you have planted the Word in your heart, it will come out of your mouth and once your words agree with God's Words you will change your circumstances and, in time, it will change your life!

Going back to Matt. 12, look at verse 36. Jesus is still speaking here and He says, "But I say unto you, that every idle word that men shall speak they shall give account thereof in the Day of Judgment." The word that has been interpreted "idle" in this verse is the Hebrew word "careless." *Webster's Dictionary* defines "careless" as "not paying enough attention; not thinking before one acts or speaks; neglectful, heedless." With this clarification, let's quote verse 36 again. "But I say unto you, that every careless word (spoken without paying attention to what you are saying and giving no heed to its consequences) you shall be held accountable for in the Day of Judgment."

Circumstances are not holding you back!

The actions of another person in your life are not holding you back!

Luck has nothing to do with it. Neither does fate.

God is not standing in your way!

Only you can effect a change in your circumstances!

Changing Your Circumstances

No matter how difficult or challenging or impossible your present situation seems to you, God has a way for you to move all the mountains of adversity out of your way and change your circumstances around to your benefit. It all begins with you. You are not in this battle alone, however. Your Heavenly Father is rooting for you; He is there to help you and give you the strength and the wisdom to make the changes in your life that are needed if you are to live in victory. One of the first things you will need to do is work toward culling the negative words out of your vocabulary and replacing them with the positive Words of God.

God wants you to prosper in every area of your life. Third John 2 gives us God's Word on it. "Beloved, I wish above all that you may prosper and be in health even as your soul prospers." God wants the very best for you. Get in agreement with Him, declare the truth of His Word, and you will discover a major key to freedom from all the negative influences in your life; freedom from every curse listed in Deut. 28. Poverty is under the curse, every illness known to man is under the curse, and Jesus redeemed us from the curse of the law. Take advantage of this gift so dearly bought and step out in the faith needed to claim all the benefits provided in the Word of God. It all begins with declaring the truth of God's Word regardless of the circumstances that surround you. Only you can bring about change in your circumstances.

Once you get your words in line with the Word of God you will align all the power and strength of our Lord who is the "High Priest" of our profession (what we say) as well as the full cooperation of the angels assigned to you and, let me tell you my friend—that mountain is going to move! Make a banner and hang it where you will see it every day.

CIRCUMSTANCES ARE SUBJECT TO CHANGE BUT GOD'S WORD NEVER CHANGES! MY WORDS CAN CHANGE MY CIRCUMSTANCES!

A Final Word About the "I" Word

I can't close this chapter without mentioning your need to watch what you say after "I" or "I'm" or what you say about "Me."

Don't bad-mouth yourself! Just keep in mind that what you say about yourself is what you will become. I've heard people say "I'm such a lost cause." Or "I'm so stupid," or "I never get good breaks," or "I'm such a klutz." Say what God says about you. Say you are a new creature in Christ Jesus, you have the mind of Christ, you have the DNA of almighty God, you can do all things through Christ who strengthens you, you have the wisdom of God, and the Holy Spirit dwells in you and teaches you all things. Don't down grade and belittle yourself. Your words are just as powerful when spoken about yourself as when declared about your circumstances.

You Can Do It; God Will Help

Work on changing your words! You can do it! Ask God to help you and before you know it you will see the obstacles in your path move aside, the challenges you face become advantages, and the truth in this chapter will be the key that opens the door to peace, financial security, health, and all the wonderful freedoms that are part of the benefits of your redemption package. These benefits belong to you as a born-again child of Almighty God because Jesus bore the curse so that the blessings of Abraham could be yours!

DEAL IN LOVE

Love the Lord your God with all your heart;
And with all your soul—emotions, will, and mind.
Then love your neighbor as you do yourself.
There's great power in love you'll find.

Love activates our faith and helps it grow;
It frees us from all stress and gives us peace.
Agape love—the love of God within our heart
Gives us joy and from burdens gives relief.

Let God's love expressed in Jesus Christ
Live in you; and very soon you'll find
Love's the only answer; the only way
Love holds the key to peace of mind.

THE FOURTH KEY

Deal in Love

Dealing in love is the foundation of our spiritual success which in turn assures us of success in every area of our lives. A catalyst activates the action of something else. Dealing in love is a catalyst to the other attributes we should exhibit as a child of God; it makes faith work; it makes our prayer life powerful and successful; it makes all the blessings of our redemption package a reality in our lives.

With any one thing being so very important to our success in life and our walk with God; we need to know all about it.

Let me begin with a review of the biblical parameters of love. In the thirteenth chapter of 1 Corinthians verses 1 through 7, a portion of 8 and verse 13, love, the agape kind of love or the God kind of love that grows in our hearts, is discussed in depth. The New International Version of the Bible is very clear and concise and to the point. Let me share that version with you first, and then we will go to the Amplified Bible because it delves into the subject more deeply and includes points that are important for us to realize as we open our minds to the richness and depth of what God is saying about love.

From NIV: "If I speak in the tongues of men and angels, but have not love, I am only a resounding gong or a clanging cymbal. If I have the gift of prophecy and can fathom all mysteries and all knowledge and if I have a faith that can move mountains, but have not love, I am nothing. If I give all I possess to the poor and surrender my body to the flames, but have not love, I gain nothing. Love is patient, love is kind. It does not envy, it does not boast, it is not proud. It is not rude, it is not self-seeking, it is not easily angered; it keeps no record of wrongs. Love does not delight in evil, but rejoices with the truth. It always protects, always trusts, always hopes, and always perseveres. Love never fails. But where there are prophesies, they will cease: where there are tongues, they will be stilled: where there is knowledge, it will pass away . . . and now these three remain: faith, hope and love. But the greatest of these is love."

The Amplified Bible leads us deeper into the subject. It refers to love as "reasoning, intentional, spiritual devotion such as is inspired by God's love for us and in us." It goes on to refer to "prophetic powers" as "the gift of interpreting the divine will and purpose of God." It further says that without love "I am a useless nobody."

Let me just quote the balance of the reference to love in the Amplified Version of the Bible. "Even if I dole out all that I have to the poor in providing food, and if I surrender my body to be burned in order that I may glory, but have not love (God's love in me), I gain nothing.

"Love endures long and is patient and kind; love never is envious nor boils over with jealousy, is not boastful or vainglorious, does not display itself haughtily.

"It is not conceited (arrogant and inflated with pride); it is not rude (unmannerly) and does not act unbecomingly. Love (God's love in us) does not insist on its own rights or its own way, for it is not self-seeking; it is not touchy or fretful or resentful; it takes no account of the evil done to it (***it pays no attention to a suffered wrong***)."

Whoa, let me repeat that last statement! "It pays no attention to a suffered wrong." That's heavy! Pays no attention, takes no account, that means ignores as if it didn't even happen.

We will get back to the rest of the Amplified Bible's insights on love. But let me insert a true story here that will exemplify what the application of love (God's love through us) can accomplish.

Dr. Kenneth Hagin Sr. was a well-known minister, writer, and educator. He established REMA Bible College in Tulsa, Oklahoma, and was a spiritual father to many that are actively in ministry today. Dr. Hagen has gone to be with the Lord, but his life and his teachings touched literally millions of lives. In a book on the subject of love, he related a story that was a perfect demonstration of how love can be applied to bring victory to any situation. A few weeks after his father passed away, he got a frantic call from his mother. She said that his siblings were waging WW III over the estate and who was going to get what. She begged Kenneth to come and intervene. He traveled to his mother's home and the morning after he arrived he heard his sister's car pull into the driveway. This was the sister who was the real instigator of all the trouble. Ken walked out on the porch. The moment she saw him his sister started screaming at him, ranting and raving about the situation and his involvement in it. It was an ugly moment, and it seemed as if it could only get uglier. Ken, however, simply stood on the porch looking at her as she worked herself into a furry. He let the love of God permeate his being and he just let that love shine through as he looked at her. In his mind, he saw them as children playing together and he was able to truly love her and let only the evidence of that love in his heart shine forth through his eyes. Suddenly she stopped ranting, looked at him, and started to cry. "Oh, Kenneth, I'm so sorry. Please forgive me. We need you, Kenneth. Please help us though this." As she said this, she fell to her knees there in the yard. Ken picked her up and just held her. Needless to say this broke the barriers that were keeping this family in total turmoil, and he was able to work through the situation to the point of settling all disagreements.

I never read that portion of scripture that I don't think of Dr. Hagin's example of applied love.

Now, let me share the rest of the verses from the Amplified Bible. We will pick up with a continued description of the attributes of love.

"It does not rejoice at injustice and unrighteousness, but rejoices when right and truth prevail. Love bears up under anything and everything that comes; is ever ready to believe the best of every person, its hopes are fadeless under all circumstances and it endures everything (without weakening). Love never fails (never fades out or becomes obsolete or comes to an end). "And so faith hope love abide (faith: conviction and belief in respect to man's relation to God and divine things; hope: joyful and confident expectation of eternal salvation; love: true affection for God and man, growing out of God's love for and in us) these three; but the greatest of these is love."

THE FOURTH KEY

The Greatest of These Is Love

The most incredible statement in this chapter describing the attributes of love is the statement made in verse thirteen, "And so abides faith, hope and love, and the greatest of these is love."

Without faith, we cannot please God; we cannot move the mountains in our lives; we cannot live in victory; we are, in fact, stymied in all areas of life. Without hope we cannot develop faith. And yet, as important as these are to our Christian walk, God is saying **love is more important**. It is the fulfillment of the law. Without it, nothing else works. It is the catalyst that makes faith work according to Gal. 5:6. Spiritual growth is impossible without love, and victory in all areas of our lives is not achievable without love. We cannot live in the fullness of our redemptive rights without love. It is a directive from Jesus Himself. He said, "This is my commandment that you love one another as I have loved you" (John 15:12).

Jesus also said to love our enemies and do good to those that despitefully use us (Matt. 5:44). It wasn't a suggestion, folks; it was a commandment.

Walk In Love

It should be unalterably clear at this point that for all the promises of God to work in our lives, we must be living in His will and His will is clearly for us to walk in love.

So how do we accomplish this?

I can almost hear you say, "It's easy for you to say, walk in love, Joy, but not very easy to do." To address that statement we will need to determine what love is and what love isn't.

What Love Is

We are not talking about love as it is depicted on your secular television screen. We do not refer to the bill of goods we have been sold that would have us believe that "love" and "sex" are synonymous. That is a total misconception and has caused more tragedy than I could possibly recount in this book. We are not speaking of romantic love found in the lovely but unrealistic "happily ever after" stories we read as children. We are talking about agape love; God's love reflected in and through us.

It is not my intent here to be redundant in going on and on about love and its true meaning, however, how can you possibly express love if you do not totally understand what the Word of God is telling us to express. So bear with me as we borrow from the *Revell Bible Dictionary* to give you some background into agape love as it sprung from the Greek interpretation and evolved to have a new and vivid meaning as we entered the era of the New Testament.

According to the *Revell Bible Dictionary*, agape (ah-gah-pay) refers to self-giving love that is not merited. During the first century, the Greek language had several different words for "love." Eros expressed the sexual side of love. Philia referred to the affection, hospitality and concern you might have for a relative or friend. Agape during this time in history was another word for love in Greek; however, its meaning was vague, and it was not often used as a noun. With the writing of the New Testament, however, the word *agape* was infused with new and stunning implications. It was used by the New Testament writers to express both the love of God and the love that knowing God infuses into human relationships.

Agape then is love as God himself has expressed it in Christ. Looking at agape in the light of God's selfless act of sacrificing His only son to atone for our sins, we must define it as completely selfless. It keeps on caring regardless of the flaws in others; it acts for the benefit of the loved one even when the act of loving cost everything. The most amazing aspect of agape is that God created the capacity for this kind of love in each believer. We have the capacity to express agape love in everything we do. We **can** express this God kind of love toward everyone that touches our lives whether they are a good person or an evil person. Eph. 5:1 says, "Be imitators of God, as dearly loved children, live a life of love, just as Christ loved us and gave himself up for us."

THE FOURTH KEY

Love In Practice

If we practice agape love, others will see God's love in us and will be drawn to the one whose love we reflect. It will reach out with a power beyond our comprehension and influence lives and touch hearts and change circumstances. Love is the most powerful force in the world.

Love is not expressed by mental assent. It is a "heart thing" not a "head thing" and the more we open ourselves up to express it, the stronger its influence on our life will be and the greater its ability to change people and situations will become.

You don't need to ask for it; it was expressed in you when you accepted Jesus as your Lord and Savior. You only need to ask your Heavenly Father to help you free the love that is within you so that it can be expressed in all ways, in all situations, and toward all men.

Love: A Key to Freedom

Why do I call understanding and expressing love in all ways, toward all people and in all the affairs of life a "Key to Freedom?"

Love is a preventor! It prevents un-forgiveness, it prevents bitterness, it eliminates stress, it prevents malice, and it prevents Satan from influencing you. It brings peace, it mends rifts, it allows you to exercise strong faith, it keeps you calm in all situations, and with all of this, it deepens you spiritually in a way that nothing else can.

Practice agape love in every aspect of your life. Whatever challenge you may face, say to yourself, "I'm going to deal in love." Approach all situations with this attitude and you will begin to understand why love is a key to personal and spiritual freedom.

Let me refer you to the words of Jesus in Matthew and John's words in Second John:

"You shall love the Lord your God with all your heart, and with all your soul, and with all your mind. This is the first and great commandment. And the second is just like it. You shall love your neighbor as yourself. On these two commandments hang all the law and the prophets" (Matt. 22:37–40).

"I say to you, Love your enemies, bless them that curse you, do good to them that hate you, and pray for them which despitefully use you, and persecute you" (Matt. 5:44).

Second John 5 and 6 (Amp) admonishes us to love one another; then verse 6 says, "And what this love consists of is this: that we live and walk in accordance with and guided by His commandments (His orders, ordinances, precepts, teaching). This is the commandment, as you have heard from the beginning that you continue to **walk in love** (guided by it and following it)." That sums it up and pretty well says it all!

It May Not Be Easy

Determine in your heart that you will **walk in love**. Is it always easy? I would be less than honest with you if I said it was easy. There will be times when Satan will try to tempt you to be angry, to entertain bitterness and even hatred. But you are more than a conqueror in Christ. Resist the temptation to react in this way. Just keep saying, "I will deal in love in this situation." Ask God to help you and as you practice the love walk it will become easier and easier until it becomes a way of life.

A major result of dealing in love is that it places you in command of any challenge you may face. It will confound your enemies. When you respond in love to negative treatment, it will baffle whoever is treating you badly. Let's say that someone is jealous of you and as a result they start a whisper campaign against you at work or in your neighborhood. You hear their car is in the shop and you offer to take them with you to the store or help them with an errand. You have just heaped coals of fire upon their head; you have shown them the love of God in action and even if it seemingly makes no lasting impression at that moment; if you will stay in love and turn the situation over to the Lord; that seed of compassion that you have sown will eventually take root. You can leave the outcome in God's hands, but your action has removed you from any emotional backwash, you will be at peace; you will not allow it to give you one moment of concern or worry. Instead of the situation putting you through an emotional wringer; you will have, by your obedience in dealing in love, removed yourself from turmoil.

Proverbs 15:1 puts it well. "A soft answer turns away wrath; but grievous words stir up anger."

James 1:19 sums up the issue completely. "My beloved brethren, let every man be swift to hear, slow to speak, slow to wrath."

Let the love of God as expressed in Christ Jesus live in you, express through you and set you free!

FORGIVEN

I've been forgiven; what a wondrous gift
Purchased for me at the cross.
My reborn spirit is all brand new
My sins blotted out at what a cost!

I've been forgiven; God so loved this world;
He gave His son to die for me.
To pay the price for my redemption;
To forgive me and set me free.

I've been forgiven and what He asks
Is that I imitate Him and forgive.
Forgive my friends; even my enemies;
It's the way I'm supposed to live.

I've been forgiven and it's not too much
To ask me to forgive in kind.
Sometimes it will be hard to do
But I've made up my mind.

I will forgive no matter what the cost.
With my Lord and Saviour by my side.
I'll strive to let all rancor go
All bitterness all pride.

I've been forgiven; so much love is mine.
So I'll let love and forgiveness flow
From God through me to others
And in my heart I know

Forgiveness as it operates through me
Will bring me blessing; will give me peace.
Will assure my prayers are answered
And will give me sweet release.

THE FIFTH KEY

Forgive, Forgive, Forgive

Forgive friends and family, forgive your enemies, forgive yourself!

I have a book in my library called *Where to Find It in the Bible, The Ultimate A to Z Resource*. The list of Bible references under the word "forgiveness" range from Genesis in the Old Testament to First John in the New Testament. We can't possible cover them all. They speak of the types of forgiveness, the need for forgiveness, God's forgiveness, forgiving grace, forgiveness as part of stewardship, the principles of forgiveness, forgiving your enemies, the need for forgiveness in prayer, the admonition to forgive members of a congregation, love and forgiveness as a prerequisite to living a Godly life, and our right to seek forgiveness through Jesus Christ who is our advocate with the Heavenly Father.

I believe that of all the scripture on the subject of forgiveness, one of the strongest can be found in Mark 11:24, 25, and 26. "Therefore I tell you, whatever you ask for in prayer, believe that you have received it, and it will be yours, and when you stand praying, if you hold anything against anyone, forgive him, so that your Father in Heaven may forgive you your sins. But if you do not forgive, neither will your Father which is in Heaven forgive your sins." Matthew 6:14 and 15, (again Jesus is speaking) basically says the same thing.

If you have been praying for something and your prayers are not being answered, check and see if you have unforgiveness in your heart.

Let's just do a quick overview on the subject of love and forgiveness in accordance with the Word of God; Lev. 19:18 tells us to love your neighbor as yourself (you can't comply with this if you haven't forgiven your neighbor); Matt. 5:44 tells us to love your enemies, bless them that curse you, do good to them that hate you, and pray for them which despitefully use you and persecute you (not possible if you don't forgive them); Rom. 13:10 tells us that love works no ill to his neighbor so love is the fulfilling of the law (anger, unforgiveness, bitterness, and a desire for revenge will stop us from living by this admonition to do no ill to our neighbor). Jesus in Matt. 18:21 and 22 tells Peter to forgive not seven times but seventy times seven. Jesus then tells His disciples the parable of the servant whose master forgave him his debts only to have him refuse to forgive *his* servant his debts. When his master found out he was angry and made that servant pay in total what was owed. After Jesus ended the parable, He said, "So likewise shall my Heavenly Father do to you if you, from your hearts, forgive not every one his brother their trespasses." I don't believe it would have been possible for Him to be any clearer on the subject. As a final reference let me direct you to Eph. 4:30, 31, and 32. "And grieve not the Holy Spirit of God, whereby you are sealed unto the day of redemption. Let all bitterness and wrath and anger and clamor and evil speaking be put away from you with all malice. And be kind one to another, tenderhearted, forgiving one another, even as God for Christ's sake has forgiven you."

It is obvious that forgiveness is a part of what God expects of us and that when we do not comply, we pay a heavy consequence.

Also I believe that by now you can begin to see why I gave "love" as a key to freedom. Love and forgiveness go hand in hand.

Why does the Word of God place so much emphasis on forgiveness?

Is there a reason that goes beyond the fact that each of us should strive to live in accordance with God's Word? Is it possible that God had something in mind beyond the need to mold and make you more like the way shower, His Son Jesus? Is there a purpose in the Bible's constant and continuous reference to your forgiving everyone and everything and treating every challenge in your life with love, kindness, patience, courtesy, and a forgiving spirit?

I believe God has our highest good in mind in telling us to even forgive our enemies and those that despitefully use us.

To understand God purpose, let's look at the results of unforgiveness.

Holding a grudge, harboring bitterness and resentment, nurturing anger and even hatred are all the end result of refusing to forgive. These emotions lead to a life of stress.

Let's take a look at what several experts on the subject of stress have to say about the outcome of all the negative emotions that stem directly from refusing to forgive and forget the wrongs that have been or are being done to us.

Pamela Harper is a certified addiction counselor, a clinical hypnotherapist, a best-selling author and a registered nurse.

In an article entitled "The Results of Anger" written by Ms. Harper on the subject she said, and I quote, "Angry people are more susceptible to disease due to the byproducts released into the system. Emotion is nothing more than an energy stimulus response which produces a bio-chemical change, these (negative) messages travel to every cell in the body. Anger in any form is self-defeating. Angry thoughts, words or deeds create a deficit in the life force. I treat people who have been angry about the same dumb darn thing for 50 years. They call it righteous indignation, or justifiable rage. They perceive that someone has wronged them and they are never going to forgive or forget. Every time they rehash that past event, a detrimental bio-chemical reaction occurs.

"Each time anger rears its ugly head and knocks you off your serene platform, it is baffling and defeating. Your stomach is in a knot, your heart rate increases, and your head may begin to ache. All of the muscles in your body are rigid. You are more likely to succumb to infection because your immune system is compromised. With a single angry thought, you can make yourself susceptible to disease."

Dr. Sarjay Chugh is a leading Indian psychologist. He sums up the results of negative emotions leading to stress in an article on the subject by saying, "A state of accumulated stress can greatly increase the risk of both acute and chronic illnesses and can weaken the immune system of the human body." According to Dr. Chugh and many other authorities on the subject, stress can cause the following:

- Headaches
- Irritable bowel syndrome
- Eating disorders
- Allergies
- Insomnia
- Backaches
- Frequent colds
- Heart ailments
- Even cancer

So let's recap:

God tells us to forgive. We cannot read His Word and deny that He admonishes each and every child of His to forgive.

Unforgiveness leads to negative emotions such as anger and bitterness, which releases chemicals into our system in harmful amounts, which in turn makes us susceptible to any and all disease.

Unforgiveness defeats our prayer life. We cannot get into a place of right standing with God (righteousness) when we refuse to forgive those who have wronged us.

So who are you hurting when you refuse to let go of hurt and angry feelings and forgive and forget?

Are you hurting the person you refuse to forgive?

No!

I'll tell you who you are hurting.

YOU ARE HURTING "YOU!"

I am reminded of a story my sister told me many years ago. She was married and living in Colorado. She owned and operated a Radio Shack. It was a few days before Christmas, and she stood thinking of how special the season was. As she gazed at the Christmas decorations inside her shop and outside on the street, which was lit up for the holidays, a woman entered the store. Nita was struck immediately by the angry look on the woman's face and the negative feeling that emulated from her. She was tiny and seemed far older than Nita later found out she was. Nita introduced herself, and before three minutes had passed, the woman began to tell Nita that the season held no joy for her because of what her husband had done to her at Christmastime. "He walked out on me for another woman and this time of year has been spoiled for me forevermore," she said with fire in her eyes. She went on to rant and rave about what an evil person her husband was. Finally, Nita asked her how many Christmases ago this had happened. The woman pondered for a moment and then said, "It's been fifty years ago this Christmas."

Was this sad angry woman hurting her ex-husband? No, he had remarried and was getting on with his life. She was only hurting herself. Nita later found out that no one wanted to have anything to do with this lady because all she ever talked about was how badly she'd been treated and how much she hated the man who had left her so many years ago. The woman later died of cancer. Do you suppose there was any connection? I don't doubt it for a moment.

I saw a sign recently that said, **"To forgive heals the wounds, and to forget heals the scars."**

It isn't always easy, but if you walk in love and seek the help of the Holy Spirit, you can do it. And let me assure you of one infallible truth: reaching a place where you can forgive and forget all past wrongs is the most freeing thing you will ever do in your life. It will seem as if the weight of the world has been lifted from your shoulders. You will ask yourself why you waited so long to take this step.

I had lunch with a dear friend just the other day, and we were discussing the subject of this message. She said she just didn't understand why anyone refused to let go of unforgiveness. She said it never ceased to amaze her that some people hold on to bitterness and resentment for years even though they are only hurting themselves. She went on to mention a friend of hers whose divorce occurred years ago. She should have been past it and getting on with her life and to all outward appearances she seemed to be doing just that. However, every time she mentioned her ex-husband she called him—not by name—but by a really derogatory name. This was an outward indication of a core of unforgiveness still lingering deep inside. We talked about the need to help her friend to forgive and forget and fill her spirit with the love of God. My luncheon companion was at a loss to understand why people don't forgive and just let go. Well, that certainly is the question of the hour.

If you are still making derogatory remarks about someone you think you have forgiven, you undoubtedly still have remnants of unforgiveness, anger and resentment in your heart. You need to root it out and let it go.

Jesus came that you might have life and have it more abundantly, that your joy might be full, that you might become more than a conqueror, that you might live in the peace that passes understanding. All this is part of your redemption package.

Is all the good that God wants for you possible with unforgiveness, bitterness, anger, and hatred in your heart? No! You will never have God's best in your life as long as you refuse to forgive and forget the hurts and wrongs of the past as well as the people who may be hurting you in one way or another right now.

About now I am sure you are thinking, "Joy, what you are saying makes sense, but I've lived with the memory of what was done to me for years. That memory and the hurt and anger I feel because of it has really become a part of me. How can I possibly root it out and just let it go?" Believe it or not, it is as easy as deciding to do it and asking God to help. I've had people say to me, "Do you mean to say that even though someone took the life of a loved one, I should just forgive them?" As hard as it may be for you to grasp this, the answer is a resounding "yes!" Will refusing to forgive the person who committed this terrible act help in any way to undo what has been done? You know it will not. All that entertaining anger, resentment, bitterness, hatred, and unforgiveness in your heart will do is slowly but surely destroy you. Do you think that is God's best for you? Do you think you can ever be happy and fulfilled and full of joy when you are carrying around all of these negative emotions? Does it solve anything? Does it hurt the perpetrator of this terrible act because you cannot forgive him or her? No to both questions. Nothing is being solved, bettered or undone by your refusal to forgive. **Only you are being hurt.** Will it be easy to let it go? Perhaps not, but with God's help you *can* forgive and let it go. It may take time for the memory to fade to the point where it is literally forgotten, however, as the sign I previously mentioned says, **"To forgive heals the wound, and to forget heals the scar."**

Let me share with you a true story. I have a very dear friend of long standing whose experience with forgiveness is extremely apropos to the issue of forgiving someone whose actions against you were heinous in nature. Before sharing this story, I asked my friend if I could do so as long as I didn't reveal her name. She agreed in hopes that the events involved would touch my readers in a meaningful way. Because of my promise to not mention her name, I will call her "Nadine" and her Mother "Rose" for the sake of clarity.

Nadine's mother had serious mental problems. I say this because no one does what Rose did if they are not mentally ill. All her early years Rose beat Nadine without any real provocation, never showed her any affection, punished her for things she did not do; and as if that wasn't bad enough, when Nadine was about twelve, Rose became jealous of her for no apparent reason and began a campaign aimed at terrorizing and ultimately killing the young girl. She would load a gun and play Russian roulette with Nadine the target. Not knowing what else to do, Nadine snuck into Rose's room and emptied the powder out of her stash of bullets. This is why Nadine is alive today; however, every time the bullets would not work because of a lack of gunpowder, Rose would go and get more bullets and the cycle of terror continued.

It was from this background of horror that Nadine was eventually rescued by a family who adopted her and gave her the love she so deeply desired and needed.

Nadine was grateful for the adopted family, but she harbored resentment and anger deep inside her being. She did not always understand her own actions because of not realizing how deeply scarred her background had left her. She was forty-one when with the help of a Christian counselor she was able to look at the unforgiveness in her heart, deal with it, and with God's help, she forgave her mother and let go of the anger and bitterness that she had harbored for so long. She just let it all go. In her own words, she told me that taking that step of forgiveness gave her a sense of freedom that she had never experienced before. She said, "If only I had taken this step sooner I could have avoided a great deal of inner turmoil and I strongly recommend to anyone reading this book that you let God help you reach a point where you can forgive the person that wronged you. When you do it will fill your heart with a new kind of freedom and it will make possible all that God has in store for you."

Before I leave the subject of forgiving the sometimes terrible things that people do let me remind you of one thing that may help you. Remember this; it is NEVER THE PERSON; it is the evil one (Satan) that is using the person to try and destroy you or whatever victim is involved. If you get fixated on the person it is difficult to justify some of the terrible things that people do—murder, harming a child, torturing someone, or any actions that fall into the "heinous crime" category. If, however, you can just keep in mind that the person doing these things is being used of the devil, granted they must be willing to be used, but it is Satan "through" the perpetrator that is doing the evil works.

Regardless of what needs to be forgiven, reaching a point where you can forgive is vital to your physical well-being and your spiritual growth. With that in mind, let me give you a *formula for forgiveness*.

1. Decide to forgive and forget all past and present hurts and wrongs.
2. Write a list of all the things that have been done to hurt you in any way for which you are harboring anger, bitterness, and unforgiveness.
3. Take that list before the Throne of Grace and ask God in Jesus name to help you forgive and forget every issue.
4. Destroy the list. Throw it in the fire, toss it in the garbage, tear it into tiny pieces, or if you have a shredder, shred it. Do this as an outward act of an inward determination to let go of the memories, let go of the bitterness, let go of the hurt, let go of all anger, and let the cleansing and healing balm of forgiveness and love heal all wounds and remove all scars.

5. Thank God that you know the truth and the truth has set you free.
6. Rejoice in your new freedom!

Forgiveness is a balm that heals a troubled spirit. Walking in love and forgiveness will set you free with a freedom that you cannot understand until you experience it.

No matter how great the wrong done to you is. No matter how hurtful, how life altering, how demeaning the act of someone in your past or present. Today I challenge you . . . ***FORGIVE THEM!***
FORGIVE THEM AND THEN LET IT ALL GO . . .

I cannot leave this subject without one last thought. Sometimes the most difficult person to forgive is you. Do you carry a burden of guilt and remorse for something you have done? Let it go. Ask God to forgive you and then forgive yourself.

I read a statement many years ago. I can't really recall which of the many books I have read that it came out of, but it eventually changed my life.

The statement went like this, "Look at your watch! The past ended a second ago. Do you have the courage to leave it there?" That says it all. In the process of forgiving yourself for past mistakes, have the courage to get on with your life. Add to that the fact that once you ask God to forgive you for whatever is haunting you from your past, it is forgiven and tossed into the sea of His forgetfulness.

I don't say "forgive yourself" glibly. I know that forgiving yourself can be even more difficult than forgiving someone else. In the early nineties, I made a bad mistake that cost me dearly. It was a bad error in judgment regarding the people I was working with. The Holy Spirit was trying to tell me that these people were not what they seemed, but I didn't want to hear that and as a result I ended up hurting myself badly and also indirectly hurting a lot of other people. I lost my business, my home, and every dime I had saved over the years. I forgave the people involved, but it took me years to finally forgive myself. In the process, I came to know that forgiveness is the only answer whether it is forgiveness of those who have harmed you or forgiveness of yourself for whatever you have done that has put you out of fellowship with God.

One day while sitting on the floor organizing my CDs, I suddenly said out loud, "Father God, do you still love me?" The answer came loud and clear in my heart, "Yes, my child, I love you and there is work for you to do." I broke down and cried for a long time and when the tears were finally over, I felt a peace settle over me that I had not known in years. If I had the forgiveness process to do over I would not have waited so long to let go of the guilt and sorrow for past sins. It accomplished nothing and only delayed the beginning of what God had in store for me.

In closing this chapter, let me ask you this. Is there a wall of unforgiveness around your heart? Have you had too much pride to make things right with your husband, your wife, your friend, your parents, your siblings, or your child? Don't let this shadow darken your life one moment longer. Pick up the phone or knock on their door—whatever it takes—and make things right. If you can't contact them directly, or you don't even know where they are because all this happened so long ago then go through the six steps I outlined above and get that demon of unforgiveness, bitterness, anger, resentment, and hatred out of your heart and its destructive influence out of your life.

The most moving example of forgiveness can be found in the Bible's recounting of Jesus' death. He had been beaten, spit upon, ridiculed, a crown of thorns placed on his head, nails driven into his hands and feet, and yet, as He hung on that cross dying the most horrible of deaths, He looked at His captors and said, "Forgive them for they know not what they do." Jesus was an example to us all to the very end. If He could forgive the terrible things that had been done to Him, surely we can follow His lead and let forgiveness become a way of life.

LOOK AT THE END RESULT OF FORGIVENESS VERSUS UNFORGIVENESS:

- **Unforgiveness** destroys the foundation of any relationship including marriage, friendship, or a business association.
- **Forgiveness** keeps a relationship strong and positive.
- **Unforgiveness** defeats us on every level.
- **Forgiveness** frees us to be our best.
- **Unforgiveness** ages us before our time.
- **Forgiveness** puts a light in our eyes and a spring in our step at any age.
- **Unforgiveness** in the long run makes us miserable.
- **Forgiveness** frees us to know joy and peace and true happiness.
- **Unforgiveness** makes us susceptible to illness and disease.
- **Forgiveness** keeps us well with a healthy immune system.
- **Unforgiveness** takes us into a state of unrighteousness.
- **Forgiveness** keeps us in right standing with God.
- **Unforgiveness** prevents us from having a successful prayer life.
- **Forgiveness** opens the doors to prayer fulfillment.

Forgiveness is the key that will open the door to a whole new world, a world full of joy and love and peace. If you have been bound by unforgiveness and the subsequent negative emotions that it inevitably leads to, then forgiveness will give you a sense of freedom you have never experienced before.

My friends, the future lies before you full of promise. Let go of the negative garbage and get on with the good life God has provided for you.

FEAR VERSUS FAITH

A child stands by a second floor window.
Looking down she sees her Daddy standing there.
"Jump Honey" he cries out, "I'll catch you."
She must jump or she won't stand a prayer.

The house is on fire and behind her
The flames have her trapped; she must now
Take a jump from the second story window;
She must have the courage somehow!

The firemen haven't arrived yet
And there's no time left, she can't wait.
With open arms her Daddy is calling;
She simply must not hesitate.

Everyone on the ground is in panic.
She's so little—surely she is afraid.
But they watch in total amazement
As she jumps; her Daddy catches her and she's okay.

Later they asked if she was scared.
She looked at them calmly and said,
"I wasn't scared of jumping 'cuz'
Daddy said he'd catch me so I went ahead.

He said he'd be there so I never thought
He wouldn't be there—not for one minute."
That is the faith of a child; and when we have it.
It banishes all fear; so let's begin it.

THE SIXTH KEY

Freedom from Fear

First John 4:18 says, "There is no fear in love; but perfect love casts out fear; because fear has torment."

Freedom from fear is a very real part of our redemption rights.

We live in a world that bombards us from every side with reasons to live in fear. Fear of the future, of what is going to happen on the political scene; of crime and its possible effect upon you and those you love; fear regarding the crumbling of financial institutions all around us; regarding our own safety and financial stability in the midst of seeming chaos. If you simply listen to the news it can send you into a state of fear.

All About Fear

Just as we defined love in the chapter on dealing in love, let's define fear. Let's look the monster in the eye, realize where it comes from; then recognize that we can conquer it and live fear free.

Fear is a SPIRIT! Second Timothy 1:7 says, "For God has not given us the *spirit of fear;* but of power and of love, and of a sound mind."

Fear is of SATAN! As we mentioned above, John 4:18 says fear has torment. This means that fear is part of the curse and the curse is Satan's domain. Satan uses fear tactics to rob you of your peace of mind. Once you entertain fear, you have opened a door for Satan to enter. James 4:7 says, "Submit yourselves to God; resist the devil and

THE SIXTH KEY

he will flee from you." Ephesians 4:27 tells us, "Neither give place to the devil." When you refuse to accept fear, you are refusing to give place to the devil.

Fear comes in all forms and in all sizes! It is insidious and hides behind what we have come to accept as part of life. For instance, *shyness is a form of fear, stage fright is a form of fear, getting shaky over heights is an obvious form of fear, fear of flying is another example. Fear of the dark, fear of disease, fear of leaving your home, fear of change, fear of strangers, fear of the unknown,* and the list goes on. There is even a type of fear that keeps the victim trapped in their own home because they are afraid to face the outside world. *Truly fear is torment.*

Let's identify fear in your own life! Are you afraid to stand up for what you believe in for **fear** of what people will say? Do you hesitate to declare the truth of God's Word because it might not be well received? Do you debate and think, "What will so and so think of me; what effect will my declaration have on my standing in the church or the social group I'm in?" *All of the above are examples of fear.*

Not all fear is sinful! There are two kinds of fear.

The first type of fear is the fear of God spoken of all through both Old and New Testaments. Fear in this context refers to honoring and having an awesome respect for God. The Word tells us this kind of fear is the beginning of wisdom because to honor and respect God indicates that we also honor and respect His Word. This kind of fear is a prelude to worship and the door to understanding that makes the wisdom of God a reality in our lives.

The other type of fear is really sin. Romans 14:23 clearly states that "what is not faith is sin." Fear is of Satan; it encompasses dread; can lead to the destruction of our peace of mind; and can eventually rob us of all the blessings contained within our redemption rights.

Fighting Fear and Winning

First John 4:18 says, "Perfect love casts out all fear." So how can love cast out fear? Perfect love is a result of perfect faith. Faith in God's covenant of protection; God's love for you; God's desire that you live in peace. Jesus said, "I come that you might have life and have it more abundantly." That hardly sounds like a fear-filled existence.

You and I are not subject to Satan—in fact, *Satan is subject to us* through the power and authority given us through the name of Jesus. You will need to bind fear and stand against it in Jesus name with full knowledge of and belief in your right to do so. Do this and Satan will back off.

You need to know that when you accepted Jesus Christ as your Lord and Savior, your spirit was reborn. At that very moment, you were delivered from the powers of darkness and translated into the kingdom of God's dear Son (Col. 1:13). We live surrounded by the world system, but we are not part of it. We are *in* it but not *of* it. God puts a wall of protection around us and unless you, by your words or actions or both, break down that wall, then the evil one cannot enter. I like to call it living in the *Embassy of God*. The American Embassy in the middle of a foreign country is under the rules and laws of America and any American citizen can find sanctuary there. *In God's Embassy we live by a new set of rules set out in God's Word and any born again Christian can find sanctuary there.*

Faith and fear cannot co-exist! Faith comes by hearing the Word of God; part of your redemption package was the issuance of a "measure of faith" and faith grows in an atmosphere of love.

We all start out with the same measure of faith. God is no respecter of persons; He didn't give me a pound of faith and you only an ounce of faith. No, *we all have the same measure of faith*. It is up to us to make that faith grow, to develop it until it becomes a power within us to defeat any enemy, move any mountain, receive from God all He has for us and claim for ourselves and our family the blessings of Abraham. It will take faith to enter into the plan God has for each of you, a plan that is for your good, a plan that involves doing His will and reaping the best of His goodness.

Faith Is the Key

How do you build perfect faith? As I said, faith comes by hearing and hearing by the Word of God (Rom. 10:17). Get in the Word, search for all the faith scriptures, and ask God to expand your understanding as you read His Word. Read several translations in order to get an even broader view of the process of having faith in God. In the chapter that follows this one, we will go into the subject of faith in more depth as we discuss claiming God's protection, but it is important to understand that there is a connection between faith, love and freedom from fear.

Let me list just a few scriptures that tell us not to fear and that the Lord has our back.

Philippians 1:28 (from the Amplified) says, "And do not (for a moment) be frightened or intimidated in anything by your opponents and adversaries for such (constancy and fearlessness) will be a clear sign (proof and seal) to them of (their impending) destruction, but a (sure token and evidence) of your deliverance and salvation that is from God."

"For in the day of trouble He (God) will hide me in His shelter; in the secret place of His tent will He hide me; He will set me high upon a rock" (Ps. 27:5).

Psalm 121 is a psalm of protection.

Isaiah 41:10 tells us not to fear.

Hebrews 13:5 and 6 is God's declaration to protect us so that we can stand against fear. It says, "He has said I will never leave you nor forsake you—so that may we boldly say, 'the Lord is my helper and I will not fear what man shall do to me."

I love Revelation 12:11, which says, "And they overcame him (refers to Satan) by the blood of the Lamb and the word of their testimony."

The ninety-first Psalm is a classic example of the many protections and blessings we have as children of the most High God. Verse 3 declares, "Surely He shall deliver me from the snare of the fowler and from the noisome pestilence" (that refers to Satan). Verse 5 says, "I shall not be afraid for the terror by night; nor for the arrow that flies by day; nor for the pestilence that walks in darkness; nor for the destruction that wastes at noonday. A thousand shall fall at my side and ten thousand at my right hand, but it shall not come nigh me . . ." Then in verse 10 it continues, "There shall no evil befall me neither shall any plague come nigh my dwelling, for He shall give his angels charge over me to keep me in all my ways; they shall bear me up in their hands lest I dash my foot against a stone." This glorious chapter goes on to promise us that God will be with us in trouble and will deliver us and honor us and satisfy us with long life. What more proof can anyone possibly need of the fact that we have a caring God who loves us and will protect us in the turns?

Please note that as I quoted the ninety-first Psalm, I used "me" and "I" instead of the neutral "thee." I do this a lot with scripture. It personalizes it for me and it becomes God speaking directly to me, my challenges, my questions and my needs. I recently read an article which said, 'The Word of God is not just a History Book or a Textbook, it is a Handbook." I think everyone should personalize scripture; it makes the text a personal journal from God the Father to you, His precious child.

Drive Out Fear with Faith

The key to overcoming fear is faith! Faith in God and His power to protect you.

Plant the Word in your heart (your spirit); soon it will begin to come out of your mouth in the words that you speak; and as that cycle is established fear will be driven out.

Perhaps the most important fact to learn in your battle with fear is that you have authority over the circumstances in your life.

I am aware that this statement may seem presumptuous; however, it is spiritually true.

In order to fully understand the issue of authority, power, or dominion (which are all words used to describe our power to control our circumstances), we need to go way back to the beginning. We covered Gen. 1:26–28 in the first chapter of this book. If you recall, in this passage of scripture, God speaks of making man in His image and after His likeness and giving him dominion over everything on the earth (the fish, the fowl, and all that creeps upon the earth). Then in verse 27 God speaks of creating man and woman and in verse 28 he blesses them and admonishes them to have dominion over every living thing upon the earth and to replenish it.

Adam was given authority and dominion here on earth. God gave him the authority and with it came the right to relinquish it and that is exactly what he did. He gave it away and Satan became the God of this earth (2 Cor. 4:4, John 12:31, and John 16:11). He is still the God of this earth, but as I mentioned before, we have been delivered from his evil and translated into the kingdom of God.

The good news in all this is that Jesus took back the authority Adam gave to Satan and gave it to you and to me. Satan's final defeat won't come until the last battle, but by the authority given to every child of God through the name of Jesus, Satan's hands have effectively been tied. He cannot harm you without your permission.

What do I mean by "without your permission"? I mean that unless you open the door with your words or actions Satan is impotent. You have a wall of protection around you and only you can create a crack in that wall. You have the authority to stop Satan in his tracks.

Exercising Your Authority

How do you exercise your authority and live victoriously which certainly includes living without fear?

I'm glad you asked.

The most important step in this process is firmly establishing in your heart and mind that you do in fact have spiritual authority on this earth—that it was originally given to Adam, that Adam relinquished it, and that Jesus (the second Adam) was given full authority in heaven and in earth and that He subsequently gave each child of God the right to live on this earth and exercise that authority in His name. God is not running things; He gave that job to you. *Please don't take my word for it, search the Scriptures, ask God through the quickening of the Holy Spirit to make this truth real to you*, and then you will be able to use your authority with confidence, and you will know how to use it effectively. Here are just a few scriptures with a re-cap of what they are saying to get you started in that direction.

BIBLICAL CONFIRMATION OF OUR SPIRITUAL AUTHORITY

- David speaks of God giving man dominion in Psalms 8:6.
- Ephesians 3:20 speaks of "the power that works in us."
- Matthew records what Jesus said just before His ascension, "All power is given unto me in heaven and in earth. Go ye therefore . . ." Then He goes on to tell them to teach and preach and that He will be with them always. In this verse, the word "power" in the Greek means "authority." So Jesus is saying that He has been given all authority and we should take that authority and do His works here on earth.
- Mark's gospel (16:15) mentions Jesus saying, "Go ye into all the world and preach the gospel to every creature." Then in verse 17, "And these signs shall follow them that believe; in my name they shall cast out devils, they shall speak with new tongues; they shall take up serpents (or exercise authority over them); and if they drink any deadly thing it shall not hurt them; they shall lay hands on the sick and they shall recover."
- Remember the results of Jesus cursing the sycamine tree? It subsequently dried up from the roots. When His disciples marveled at this Jesus tells them in Luke 17:6 that if they have the faith of a mustard seed, they could even command the tree to be cast into the sea, and it would obey them.
- In Luke 10:19, Jesus tells His disciples that He has given them power (in the Greek this means authority) over all the power of the enemy and nothing will hurt them. He goes on in verse 20 to say that the spirits are subject to us in His (Jesus) name.
- Jesus tells His disciples (and you and me) in John 14:12 that the works that He has done we will do and "greater works that these shall you do . . ." In verse 13 Jesus says that whatever you ask in His name He will do which speaks to the power and authority in His name. Jesus is

saying here that we can use this authority. (This scripture speaks of "works" not petition prayer which is approached in a different way.)

- The classic scripture for the power of words is Mark 11:23 and 24; however it is also a strong statement for the extent of our authority. *We* can *move the mountains in our lives.*
- Acts 19:13–17 tells the story of an exorcist named Sceva and his seven sons. This family lived in Ephesus, which biblical history tells us was given over to the occult so that demonic activity was rampant. These men had not accepted Christ and so were not born again members of the family of God. They took it upon themselves to "exorcize" the evil spirits in a certain man. In their infinite wisdom and ego, they said, "We adjure you by Jesus whom Paul preaches." They learned a great lesson that day, because the evil spirit said to them, "Jesus I know, and Paul I know, but who are you?" All seven of those men who tried to act without the authority to do so, ended up naked and wounded. This confirms that the authority only belongs to those of us who are part of the family of God.

We Are Redeemed from Fear!

Jesus speaks of Himself as the "ransom" for many. His sacrifice redeemed us from the curse of the law 'so that the blessings of Abraham might come on the Gentiles through Jesus Christ (Gal. 3:13, 14). The curses of the law (Deut. 28, from verse 14 on) are orchestrated by Satan but *as long as we live in accordance with God's will (God's Word is His will) and accept our full redemption we are redeemed from every single curse.*

We are told to "resist the devil and he will flee from you" (James 4:7).

Once these truths are a reality in your life, you will stand against anything bad that Satan tries to throw at you. You will stand against it in Jesus name and you will become "more than a conqueror in

Christ" (Rom. 8:37). "No weapon formed against you will prosper" (Isa. 54:17).

Peter Began to Sink?

I'm reminded of the story of Peter when he walked on the water toward Jesus. In Matt. 14:29, it says, "And when Peter was come down out of the ship, he walked on the water to go to Jesus."

Peter walked on the water! He paid no attention to the circumstances or the laws of nature that would preclude anyone walking on water as if it were a hard surface; he didn't give a thought to the waves or the wind or the impossibility of what he was doing; he just kept his eyes on Jesus and walked right out there on the water to go to Him.

Then in verse 30 it says, "But when he *saw* the wind boisterous, he was afraid; and began to sink." He took his eyes off Jesus, got them on the circumstances, and two things happened. First, faith vanished because he let fear in, and secondly, he *"began to sink."*

I have always found that phrase mind boggling. **Began to sink!** Nobody *"begins"* to sink; if you step out on water you go down like a rock. To me, it says that fear is insidious and its effects are sometimes slow in showing themselves. Fear is a negative emotion that can—over time—affect you physically, mentally, and spiritually.

The moral of Peter's story is *"keep your eyes on Jesus;"* on the power and authority that works in you and no circumstance will defeat you.

Fighting the Good Fight of Faith

First Timothy 6:12 tells us to "fight the good fight of faith." It's a good fight because we have the wherewithal to win in Christ; however what I want to point out to you about this scripture is this—*faith is a fight!*

Many Christians come into the faith expecting it to be smooth sailing from that point on. *Not so!* God does not say it will be a walk in the park with no opposition. We have an adversary and he would

THE SIXTH KEY

very much like to destroy you. *The good news is that he is powerless as long as we realize that we are "more than conquerors in Christ."* Jesus overcame the Satan issue long ago and once you come into the knowledge of your authority in Christ and your privileges as a child of God you will begin to stand against the devil's efforts to defeat you—*and you will win!*

Faith Versus Fear

Fear is the antitheses of faith! They are opposite sides of the coin and in effect *you can't live in fear and have faith;* in the same way *you can't live in faith and have fear.* Faith eliminates fear just like light eliminates darkness. Darkness can't exist when light fills the room and *fear can't exist when faith fills our hearts.*

The development of your faith then becomes of vast importance. Once your faith in God's Word is strong within you it should be more than possible for you to take the next step and claim God's protection of yourself and your loved ones.

We will be talking about claiming God's protection in the next chapter.

THE WALL, THE WORD, AND THE ANGELS

There's a wall of protection around me;
It protects me everywhere that I go.
It protects not only me but my family;
I can't see it but it's there I know.

I use God's Word to activate
The protections I've been given.
I plead the blood; I speak the Word,
And in Jesus name I can move Heaven.

I have angels that surround me.
To protect me and those I hold dear.
Thank God for the ministry of angels.
I always sense their presence near.

The Holy Spirit guides my steps;
He'll keep me out of harm's way.
As I grow sensitive to His guidance;
He will lead me through each day.

He will warn me if there's danger;
He'll keep me safe from harm.
It's one more way I'm protected.
I have no reason for alarm.

The wall, the Word, the angels
And the Holy Spirit's intervention;
All keep me safe, protect me and mine.
And assure me of disaster prevention.

THE SEVENTH KEY

Claim God's Protection

Do you have the right to God's protection? Do you have the authority to claim protection for your family? Can you prevent disaster from striking you or your loved ones?

The answer to all of the above questions is . . . **YES!**

Let's find out how to do it and what Biblical basis to stand on.

Claim the Blood and Listen to Your Inner Witness

We have the right to plead the blood of Jesus with its power to separate from the curse of sin and death. Revelations 12:10 and 11 speaks of the "accuser of the brethren" (that would be Satan) being cast down and as a result of his defeat, verse 11 states that we have "overcome him (Satan) by the blood of the lamb and the word of our testimony."

The blood Jesus shed at Calvary covers sin and the entire curse, and that includes anything Satan tries to throw at you or your family.

I never leave my home that I don't plead the blood over our trip, ourselves, and our home while we are gone. I have seen the resultant protection save me (or whatever member of my family I use it for) time and time again. I have seen accidents prevented by miraculous means, dangerous situations defused, catastrophes prevented because I have pled the blood and listened to my inner witness.

If I have a sense in my spirit not to take a planned trip; I change my plans. If something delays me for seemingly no reason; I thank

God that I have been rescued from something that would have happened if I had not had the oft time annoying delay.

I will give you just one example of a delay that saved not only my life but the life of my entire family. My mom and dad and I were traveling across the Arizona dessert when the car over-heated, boiled over and steam spouted out from under the hood. Dad got out and opened the hood but the water cap was far too hot to touch so we did the only thing we could do—we waited. After about thirty minutes, it cooled down enough that we could limp into the next service station, which thankfully was just over the hill where we had stopped. We coasted into the station and while dad dealt with the water tank issue mom and I went into the little café that was next to the service station. Everyone was glued to the radio (this was a long time ago) listening to a special news report of a private plane that had crashed on the highway a few miles up the road that we were on. We later calculated that if we hadn't been delayed by the car over heating we would certainly have been on the exact spot where the plane crashed. We went out to tell all this to my dad and found him shaking his head. It seems the car did not need any water; there was absolutely nothing wrong with it, and once the road had been cleared for travel, we continued on our way and the car never overheated again.

We had pled the blood of Jesus over that trip, the car, and each of us. As the old song says, "There is Power in the Blood."

Many stories came out of the 9/11 tragedy regarding those who were delayed, in some cases for odd reasons, and were not there when the attack took place.

There were also a number of stories of those who felt in their spirits that they should stay home that day; those that listened to that inner witness lived to tell about it.

I knew of a minister who had several near fatal accidents. He later admitted that each time he had been told in the spirit to wait and seek God about his plans and each time he ignored the warning because he didn't think he had time to spend in prayer before leaving for his appointments. Finally it dawned on him that his failure to listen was giving Satan a crack in the wall of protection that God puts around each of us. The next time he felt a "tic" in his spirit about his plans, he changed his plans. No more near misses.

Let me ask you a question. Would a loving father allow his son or daughter to walk into a situation in which their safety and perhaps even their lives were at risk? Wouldn't he at least warn them of the dangers involved? If you are a parent wouldn't you take steps to prevent something catastrophic happening to your child if you had it in your power to do so? I believe you would, so why would anyone think that our Heavenly Father wouldn't warn us of impending danger?

Learning to Listen to Your Inner Witness

If your spirit has been reborn, it is a reliable guide because it is under the influence of the Holy Spirit. God indwells your spirit by the unction of the Holy Spirit. He will speak to your reborn spirit man, which relays what has been said to your conscious mind. This kind of direction and instruction comes from within. It has been called a "still small voice" or "conscience." It is not an audible voice, but you will know it because it comes from within out. Satan's voice comes from without directly to your mind but the Holy Spirit speaks to your mind through your reborn spirit.

The mind is the door or gateway through which your spirit speaks to you from within and the only portal through which Satan can enter and only if you allow him to do so. You will need to learn to discern the difference between the leading of your spirit and the suggestions of the evil one.

Once we have been born again it is up to us to "work out our salvation." Does that seem contradictory? You are a three-fold being—you *are* a spirit, you live in a body, and you have a soul which is your mind, will, and emotions (1 Thes. 5:23 and 1 Peter 1:9). We are told to renew our mind. The mind of man is renewed with the Word of God. Once renewed, your mind will judge everything suggested to it in accordance with the Word of God. Guard your mind; stand against Satan's attempts to mislead you and only listen to the still small voice of your inner man (your spirit). A mind renewed with the Word of God will not be easily led down the wrong path and will be sensitive to any warning given.

Your Protective Mechanism

Part of your protective mechanism involves becoming sensitive to the inner witness. Ask God to help you learn to listen with your inner ears for the direction of the Holy Spirit. He will guide you through your inner man – your spirit man – the real you that has been re born and infused with the attributes and the wisdom of your Heavenly Father.

Once you have learned to sense the leading of God through your spirit; and once you determine to follow that leading; then the Holy Spirit can warn you in the event of impending danger; deal with you regarding the affairs of life; and guide you in the direction God would have you take in order for you to be in His perfect will.

Protection from all harm is part of your covenant rights; part of your redemption package; and available to you if you are willing to put forth the effort to make yourself sensitive to the leading of the Holy Spirit.

You Have Angels to Protect You

In the first chapter of Hebrews, the Apostle Paul in speaking of Jesus being the express image of God indicates that the angels of God worship him. In verse 14, he says, "Are not the angels all ministering spirits sent out in the service of God for the assistance of those who are to inherit salvation?" We are the ones who have inherited salvation and there always has been and always will be a ministry of angels.

There are good angels and bad angels but that is another book. Actually a book has been written on the subject by Charles and Annette Capps and it is amazing. Do read it sometime. But we are talking about the good angels assigned to you by your Heavenly Father, assigned to minister to you, to serve you, and to protect you.

Angels are spoken of all throughout the Bible. This vital ministry did not die out with the new covenant, but if you make a trip and upon your arrival are asked how the trip went and you say, "It was a great trip and a safe one because my angels take care of me," you will likely be looked at askance. Regardless of their reaction, however, it is a true statement.

If you research the Old Testament for the mention of angels, you will find them everywhere. They appeared to Abraham, Lot, Jacob, Moses, Joshua, Gideon, David, and all the prophets. I love the story in 2 Kings 6:8–23. The forces of the King of Syria had the compound of Elisha the Prophet surrounded. When his servant saw the vast army surrounding them, he totally panicked and ran in terror to Elisha. Elisha told the young man not to be afraid because "they that be with us are more than they that be with them." I'm sure the servant thought he'd lost it, but then Elisha asked God to "open the servant's eyes (that would be his spiritual eyes)" and then it says in verse 17, "And the Lord opened the eyes of the young man; and he saw; and behold *the mountain was full of horses and chariots of fire round about Elisha.*" What he saw were warrior angels. What a great God we have!

In the gospels, an angel appeared to Mary regarding the birth of Jesus; to Joseph to tell him what had happened and later to warn him to leave for Egypt to escape those that would try and kill Jesus.

Angels appeared to the shepherds at the birth of our Lord, to Mary Magdalene at his tomb, and later to many of the Apostles including Paul, Peter, Philip, and John.

They appeared to Cornelius to tell him to seek Peter in order to find out how he and his household might be saved.

This list is endless. With all this angelic activity, why would we think this protective ministry is no longer available to us as children of God?

Activating our Angels

So how do we activate our angels and take advantage of their help and protection?

They are activated by your words (Psalms 103:20); that is why it is so important to keep the Word of God in your mouth. If you tell your angels to protect you, your loved ones, your home, your activities IN JESUS' NAME; you can plan on them going into action. Your protection is part of the blessings of Abraham that were passed down to you; so your request for protection is in line with the Word of God. They are assigned to act for you as long as what you say is not contrary to God's Word.

This is why the constant admonition to watch what we say—that we will be accountable for idle words, that we will have what we say, that if we abide in Him and His words abide in us we can ask anything, and it will be done. God designed the angels to hearken to the voice of his Word (Psalms 103:20).

I could tell you a number of stories regarding the ministry of angels in the earth today, but two that I know of stand out in my mind so I'll share them with you in the hopes that you will start to take advantage of the protection available to you through the ministry of angels.

The first story happened years ago. The minister of a church in a bad section of a metropolitan city set out to bring down the local crime lord who was targeting young people and was dealing in drugs. Over a period of time, this crime syndicate leader became enraged over the campaign that the minister was heading and swore to put him out of operation.

One evening, after a young people's meeting at the church, the minister decided to walk home through the city park. He lived on the other side of the park and said he needed the walk to clear his head. The elders offered to go with him because of all the threats he had been receiving over his efforts against the crime lord, but this man refused to live in fear, and whether it was wise of him or not, he left the church and headed for the park. He got home safely and gave no further thought to the incident until several years later when the man he had waged a campaign to bring down was at death's door and called for him. As the minister stood by his hospital bed, the man told him that he had hidden in the bushes that night in the park with a gun tucked under his coat. "I fully intended to kill you!" he said.

"What stopped you?" the Minister asked him. His answer will rock you—it did me. He said, *"I couldn't take the chance because of all those big guys you had with you."*

The other story is one that was told to us during a meeting at the church I am presently attending. A woman shared with us the harrowing story of being attacked during her early morning walk by a naked man that she couldn't even stop with mace spray. As she fought for her life, she remembered that the Word of God said she had the power to bind and loose in the name of Jesus. She pointed her finger at her assailant and shouted at him, "I bind you in the name of Jesus Christ!" The man put his hands on his head, looked at an area over her head, and took off as fast as he could run. She did not say so, but I think there is no doubt he saw her angels and it scared him into a fast retreat. Thank God that she remembered she had the right to bind evil and the presence of mind to do so.

I could take up the rest of this book with stories about the intervention of angels on behalf of the children of God, but I think the point has been made. We do have angels that are here to guard and protect us. Let's take advantage of this God provided ministry of angels.

The Word of God is full of protection promises. Search for them; they will not be hard to find. Start with Psalms 91 in its entirety and Psalms 103:1–5.

Let's Recap

You have at your disposal everything you will ever need to live under the protection of God and to protect not only yourself but your family.

Let's recap the procedure:

1. Use your right to *plead the blood of Jesus* over yourself and those you love. Do it on a daily basis.
2. *Develop a sensitivity to the Holy Spirit,* which in dwells you. Part of the steps you need to take to do this involves

becoming well acquainted with the Word of God so that you will be able to discern whose voice you are hearing. Whatever your spirit under the direction of the Holy Spirit tells you will agree with God's Word. Praying daily in the Spirit will also help you to become sensitive to your inner witness. As your ability to hear inner direction develops, listen and immediately do what you are being told to do or don't do what you are being told not to do. In this way, you will open yourself to being warned of danger and protected from all harm.

3. *Take advantage of God's ministry of angels.* Tell your angels to go with you and protect you and they will act on your behalf to stand between you and danger. Remember that they "hearken to the voice of His word" so watch your words.

You can walk in the protection provided as part of your redemption rights. There is a wall of protection surrounding you as long as you don't do or say anything to jeopardize that wall.

It's all up to you—***the key to divine protection is in your hands!***

MYTH

A Myth according to Webster
Is a story we've come to accept;
But it's really only a theory
Past generations have kept.

Passed down from one to the other
It takes a firm grip and you'll find
That only the truth can root it out.
That and an open receptive mind.

Myths lead to misconceptions
And mixed in the muddle there'll be
A pack of misinformation
Enough to confuse you and me.

The truth of God's Word is the answer.
Let's study to rightly divide
The truth that's been so richly given;
Plant the seeds of that truth deep inside.

Water those seeds and watch them
Send their roots deep into your spirit.
Faith will develop as you speak the Word;
Listen to the Word you must hear it.

For faith comes by hearing and hearing
And the knowledge of God's Word sets you free.
As it grows in your heart you will speak it.
And then you will have the eighth key.

THE EIGHTH KEY

Clearing Up Myths, Misconceptions, and Misinformation

As we embark on this all important issue of myths, misconceptions, and misinformation, it is vital that we look at the conditions at the time of Jesus' life on earth as they relate to the prevalent condition of Christians today.

Jesus was born to a people who had, for the most part, forgotten what the blessings of Abraham were. As a result, they were living under the influence of Satan's curse. They suffered from every kind of illness—from demon possession, from extreme poverty, and from a lack of real hope for the future. Their lame begged by the side of the road and their children died young. They had just come through four hundred years without a prophet, had lost their will to stand against the evil that Satan had brought upon them, and except for just a small nucleus of those that still were true to God and His commandments, they had given up hope of a Messiah and had caved to Roman tyranny.

It is one thing to know the Bible, but it is quite another thing to know the God of the Bible!

The scribes, priests, Pharisees, and Sadducees of Jesus' day knew the Torah, but they did not know the God of the Torah. They knew the law but mocked and made it of no effect with their lives and their actions. They steeped themselves in traditional minutia and overlooked the blessings of Abraham given by God through Abraham to them. They strained at a gnat and swallowed a camel. They were so caught up in their own sense of importance that they wanted no part of anyone that would upset the status quo of their selfish, self-centered lives, which depended on the approval and praise of men. As a result, they once again turned away from their promised land and crucified their own Messiah. Jesus was the promised Savior that their own prophets had pointed to throughout their own Torah. Here was the promise of a new covenant—a better covenant, a life lived in victory and peace and harmony; but in the same way that their ancestors turned away from the promised land because of the unbelief in their hearts, so these leaders turned their backs on the doctrine of Jesus Christ because it did not agree with their preconceived hidebound concepts of "the law." How sad—how more than sad—how tragic!

And yet their actions are a prototype of what many Churches and many Christians are doing today. They are so steeped in tradition based on what they think the Bible said instead of what the Bible actually "said" that they are turning away from the blessings of Abraham given them through the sacrificial death of Jesus. As a result, they are suffering the effects of the curse because they have rejected what Jesus paid the final price to make available to them and thus, in effect, they have denied Christ himself.

Matthew speaks of those that are walking in darkness in chapter 6:23 and says if the light in you be darkness, how great is that darkness. So many Christians today fit that picture. I am reminded of what is said in Hosea 4:6, "My people perish for lack of knowledge."

Someone in a church meeting I recently went too said to the group of people he was with, "Satan is really beating up the children of God." I overheard and interrupted him. I said, "And we're letting him. We should be standing against Satan and binding him in Jesus name. Satan has no authority to attack the children of God." The man looked at me in amazement. He was amazed because he didn't have a clue what I meant.

It is important to remember that the Bible is not just a history book, and it's not even just a textbook—it is a handbook. It is a handbook for living victoriously in Christ. We need to read its instructions carefully in the areas where there has been confusion resulting in misinformation being disseminated resulting in even more confusion. As an example, the tragic truth is that many honest sincere Christians are living under the curse because they have the mistaken idea that it is God's will for them to do so.

Let's clear up some of these misguided ideas; let's find out what the Word of God really says instead of what Uncle Ralph or Aunt Tilley told us it said. Of course, sometimes misinformation actually comes from the pulpit, but regardless of where it came from, once you understand the truth, as Jesus said, "If you continue in my word, then are you my disciples indeed; and you will know the truth and the truth shall make you free" (John 8:31–32).

This book has been written in a sincere effort to free you to be all that God longs for you to be.

This is a huge subject so I am going to cover one issue at a time by breaking this chapter into parts. In this way, you can cover a section and then take time to double check all the scriptures used to validate what has been said.

Part I: The Sickness Issue

Question: Is it true that God uses sickness to teach us?

Answer: **No, that is not true!** Let's go to the Word of God and find out how God corrects his children. According to 2 Tim. 3:16, "All scripture is given by inspiration of God and is profitable for doctrine, for reproof, for correction, for instruction in righteousness (the right way of doing things)."

Let's go to the scripture that has become a stumbling a block to some Christians who think that God makes us sick or brings calamity on us in order to teach us some profound something.

"My son, do not despise or shrink from the chastening of the Lord; neither weary of his correction; for whom the Lord loves he corrects; even as a father the son in whom he delights" (Prov. 3:11 and 12).

This scripture tells us three things: first, we should be open and receptive to God's discipline and His correction; second, we can plan on His discipline and correction being done in love as a father would correct a son in whom he delights; and lastly, the loving manner in which God corrects us according to this scripture precludes the use of sickness to correct us. Sometimes, when God deals with us through his Word, it can be hard to take; we must realize that it is for our growth and our highest good. His discipline, however, will come from His Word, not by making us sick or leading us into calamity. That would hardly be the actions of a father who delights in and loves his child.

Would a good earthly father deliberately infect his beloved son with a disease that will make him suffer physically and perhaps even die in order to teach him something? I don't think so! Why then would we think that God who IS LOVE would use such a method to correct his beloved child?

Remember, God is in the healing business, not the sickness business, so He is never going to be the author of sickness and disease.

I read recently in a commentary that "Healing glorifies God and gives Him a wider use of your life in His service." That made perfect sense to me.

Jesus Taught and Healed

Jesus did two major things while He was on earth; He taught and He healed all that were "oppressed of the devil" (Acts 10:38). His healing ministry was legend; no matter where He went, He healed, and time after time, He referred to Satan being the cause of the illness. It also said He came to destroy the works of the devil. This should make it very clear that Satan is the author of sickness and disease, not God. Sickness is clearly delineated as part of the curse that was brought on the earth through Adam's sin, which gave Satan the authority to do just what he had been doing until Jesus took that authority back and subsequently gave it to you and to me.

Does it make any sense at all that God, who is the same yesterday today and forever, who changes not and for whom there is no shadow of turning, would contradict all that He is and make you sick so that you could somehow learn from the experience? Again, I don't think so!

I've had so many people say to me when I present this truth to them, "Yes, but Joy, it was only when I was in the hospital that God was able to reach me and I made a commitment to give him the rest of my life." Will God take a situation that YOU HAVE GOTTEN YOURSELF INTO and turn it around for your good? Yes He will—every time, if you will let Him do so. That does not mean He caused the situation, the trouble, the disaster, or the sickness.

At this point, you may question what I mean by "a situation that you have gotten yourself into." We as Christians have been wrongly blaming God for every bad thing that has happened to us. We've been doing so for so long that the concept that we just might be responsible for the disasters, the illnesses, and the problems we either face or have gone through is totally foreign to us.

It's time for the truth. It's time to take the reins of your life and steer your ship in the right direction—in God's direction.

I heard a minister of the Gospel ask why so and so was sick and why God heals some people and not others. I have often wondered if that particular minister really wanted to know the answer. He's been putting the blame on God for so long that a turnaround will be difficult for him.

There is an answer, and it is not a simple one because each case will vary and depend upon many things that we may not know about the person who is suffering an illness perhaps even to death.

We would need to know the following:

1. Are they aware that their body is the temple of the living God? (1 Cor. 6:19). If so have they been treating it as such? Have they applied the rules of good nutrition to what they eat and what they serve their family? Is their lifestyle health-oriented? Are they eating nutritional food, getting enough exercise, are they weight conscious, etc.? If you buy a brand-new car, neglect to have it serviced, give it substandard fuel and cheap oil, and it starts to have

mechanical problems, do you blame the manufacturer? Of course not and yet many people ignore the nutritional needs of their God-given bodies, and when they break down, they blame God. Go figure!
2. Have they spoken the truth of God's Word into their circumstances or do they constantly declare the negative? If their words are continually in direct contradiction to the Word of God then what they are saying may very well be coming to pass in their lives.

Regarding the issue of speaking God's word into their circumstances, let me give you an example. The Word of God promises the following regarding healing:

Acts 10:38: Sickness is called an "oppression of the devil."

Psalms 103:3: God forgives all our iniquities and "heals all our diseases."

Isaiah 53:5: Isaiah's prophetic utterance tells us that "with his stripes we are healed."

1 Peter 2:24: Isaiah's prophesy is fulfilled in this passage which says, "By whose stripes you were healed."

Matthew 10:1: Jesus tells His disciples to "heal all manner of sickness and all manner of disease."

Luke 5:17–26: Jesus heals the man with palsy.

Mark 5:22–42: Jesus heals Jairus's daughter and the woman with the issue of blood.

Matthew 8:7 & 13: Jesus heals the centurion's servant.

Luke 6:19: Jesus "healed them all."

Malachi 4:2: Speaks prophetically of the "Sun of righteousness" coming with healing in his wings. That prophesy was fulfilled in Jesus.

Exodus 15:26: God tells Moses (and you and I), "I am the God that healeth thee."

This list is only a small part of the scriptures on healing.

With all this evidence of God's willingness and desire to heal you, considering the known fact that Jesus' ministry involved teaching and healing and He was called the great healer; if you continue to use "sick," "death," "killing," "tired," words as figures of speech, you are talking contrary to God's Word and His will for you. This type of speech is called "idle words" in Matt. 12:36 and "corrupt communication" in Eph. 4:29. If you think this doesn't apply to you because you don't use these words in any such manner, just give yourself a day or two and listen—really listen to what you are saying. If you never hear yourself say, "I'm sick and tired of such and such," "My feet are killing me." "This (piece of pie or something else you enjoy) is to die for," or "I'm just dying to do such and such," then I commend you for being perfect because James says in James 3:2 that anyone that can bridle their tongue is a perfect man (or woman).

Even if you fall into the "perfect" category, you may still be talking *ABOUT* the mountain instead of talking *TO* it. What do I mean by this? Mark 11:22, 23 tells us to speak to the mountains in our lives whether that mountain is sickness, poverty, or chaos. If we believe in our hearts that the mountain will move and continue to say with our mouth that it will then IT WILL MOVE. But if we just talk about how big the mountain is and we wonder what to do about it, then it isn't going anywhere and the more we talk about it the bigger it is going to get. This analogy works with any challenge in our lives.

We cannot leave this subject without addressing the issue of faith. If you need healing, you need to build your faith for healing. Faith comes by hearing and hearing by the Word of God. Saturate yourself in healing scriptures until the concept of God healing you becomes so real you cannot image that he will *not* heal you. This kind of faith can bring the miraculous into play in your situation regardless to what extent you have caused the illness through neglect of your body or to what extent your words have been contrary to the Word of God. Let me assure you that God has not gone out of the miracle business.

So back to the answer to the question of why did sister or brother so and so get sick and why didn't God heal them. There is no pat answer, but this I know; somewhere in the answers to the questions I have posed is the reason they got sick in the first place and why they didn't receive their healing. Perhaps they were unaware that divine healing was part of their redemption package and that what they needed to do was claim it in Jesus' name and stand against any symptom that Satan tried to put on them. Perhaps they didn't realize that their words were stout against the Word of God and were opening the door for Satan to do what he does best. The Word says he came to kill, steal, and destroy and he is the great deceiver. Perhaps they were unaware of their authority in the name of Jesus and that they could tell Satan to take a hike in Jesus' name, and he would take off in terror. Maybe they didn't read in the Word of God where Jesus took back the authority from Satan that he got illegitimately from Adam and made a show of the dude openly. Now the only way Satan can have a say on earth is to find a person that will let him work his evil through them.

Just know this; it is God's will to heal—He is the healer, sickness is part of the curse, we've been redeemed from the curse, and with that being scripturally true, we have to face the cold hard fact that if healing is not operating in our lives it is not God's fault so it must be ours.

Part II: The Calamity Issue

Questions:

1. If God is a good God, why does He let bad things happen to good people?
2. Is it true that God brings calamity our way to help us grow spiritually?

Answer:

Ah, yes, the eternal cry of why do bad things happen to good people. I believe the answer to that will emerge as we discuss who causes calamity and who is responsible for supposed "acts of God".

James 1:13 referring to temptations, trials, and tests specifically states that God is not the author. That's Satan's territory. Plus, in my opinion, many of the disasters in our lives could have been prevented.

In the chapter before this one, we discussed claiming God's protection which really covers what is needed in order for you to protect yourself and your loved ones from the efforts of Satan to destroy you. I believe we firmly established that it is Satan who comes to steal, kill, and destroy, not God; and we have also determined that God teaches His children through His word NOT by bringing sickness or calamity on us.

Let's cover the types of calamity that are caused by natural forces on the rampage, and let's establish once and for all who causes them. Hurricanes, tornados, tidal waves, and any other destructive examples of nature at her worst are not acts of God. They are examples of Satan distorting nature, and as children of God, we do have recourse against such acts of the devil. I could give you story after story of people who have survived these types of disaster either by taking protective steps on a spiritual level or because they were warned, were attuned to the inner witness of the Holy Spirit and avoided the disaster entirely.

Let's Look at the Word of God on the Subject of Protection.

The 101st Psalm promises that God will deliver our life from destruction. The 91st Psalm is the classic Psalm of protection, but that protection is based on "dwelling in the shadow of the most high." In other words, walking in accordance with the Word of God is a prerequisite for taking advantage of God's protection.

Let me now point you to three scriptures (in the mouth of three witnesses shall every word be established).

Matthew 16:19 says, "I will give unto thee the keys of the Kingdom of heaven and whatsoever thou shall bind on earth shall be bound in heaven; and whatsoever thou shall loose on earth shall be loosed in heaven."

Matthew 8:23–26 says, "And when He (Jesus) was entered into a ship, His disciples followed Him, and behold, there arose a great tempest in the sea in so much that the ship was covered with the waves; but He was asleep. And His disciples came to Him and awoke Him saying, Lord save us; we perish; and He said unto them, 'Why are you fearful, O you of little faith?' then He arose and rebuked the winds and the sea and there was a great calm."

John 14:12 says, "Verily, verily, I say unto you; he that believeth on me the works that I do shall he do also and greater works than these shall he do because I go unto my Father."

Doing the Greater Works

I can almost hear you pose the question, "Are you saying, Joy, that we can do even greater things than Jesus did? Are you trying to tell us we can change the course of a tornado, for instance? If that is what you are saying, you must be kidding!"

My answer is, "Yes, we can do what Jesus did *in Jesus' name*. Yes, we could bind the tornado and send it on its way *in Jesus' name*, and no, I am definitely not kidding."

That is what Jesus said and red words win. I didn't say it, *Jesus said it!* If Jesus said it, I believe it, and that—for me—settles it.

I have personally known of an instance where a tornado tried to strike the property of a born-again child of God who knew the extent of their authority in Christ; they pointed to the tornado and told it in Jesus' name to get away from them and their property. I heard this from someone who was with them at the time and they said, "As God is my witness that black, tunnel-shaped beast paused and then turned and headed in the opposite direction!"

In the wake of hurricane Katrina, one family that knew their rights in Christ ordered their angels in Jesus' name to stand at the four corners of their home and protect them. I saw the photographic proof of devastated homes in the entire area with the exception of theirs, which was untouched.

As far as doing the works of Jesus, that is what Acts is all about—His disciples doing the works of Jesus and that is what we are supposed to be doing. The day pastors start getting a few people raised from the dead, they won't have to be concerned about filling their churches because people in need of God will be standing in line to get in.

That is what we are supposed to be—ambassadors for Jesus Christ, with signs following. The Word says Jesus was "the first born of many brethren"(Col. 1:15). We have the authority in the name of Jesus to do what He did.

Don't ask, "Is it possible?" Ask, "Why isn't it happening?" Why aren't we seeing the miracles that followed Jesus and the apostles? It isn't because it's not possible; it is because we haven't come into the full knowledge of our place in Christ and our authority in His name.

So let's get into the Word and build our faith for all that has been made available to us because we have been born again and have inherited the blessings of Abraham and have been given full authority to act in Jesus' name.

Part III: The Prosperity Issue

Questions:

1. Does God expect me to give up everything material to follow Him?
2. Doesn't the Bible teach that money is the root of all evil?
3. Jesus was our way shower and doesn't the Bible say he was poor?

The answer to all three of these questions is a resounding "NO!"

Let's deal with these questions by looking to God's Word for the answers that will clarify things for you.

If you have read through the list of curses in Deut. 28 from verse 15 on, you must know that poverty is a curse. Gal. 3:13 and 14 states that we have been redeemed from the curse of the law through Jesus sacrifice at Calvary; it goes on to state that we have been given the blessings of Abraham, which are listed in verses 1 through 13 of Deut. 28.

Jesus paid with his life to redeem you, not only from sin and sickness but also from poverty and mental torment, so why in the world would he want you to suffer what he has redeemed you from?

THE EIGHTH KEY

In Mark 16:15, Jesus' parting words to his disciples and to you and me was, "Go ye unto all the world and preach the gospel to every creature." This admonition to spread the gospel was also reported in Matt. 28:19. How are we to do this without the financial wherewithal to send missionaries, without the money to keep churches open, and without the funds to utilize a media outreach to reach those that might not go to church?

The misguided concept that God wants his children poor and barely making it financially is a lie right out of the pit of hell. Satan would love to keep you poor; you are less likely to support the ministry.

The Bible is full of the stories of those who were rich because God richly blessed them. From Abraham who, as we said earlier in this book, was rich in land, in gold, and in silver; to Isaac whom God richly blessed; to David whose kingdom was great; to Solomon who surpassed his Father in wealth; and on through the Old Testament, we are told that God blessed His people.

Perhaps you thought that because Jesus said, "blessed be the poor in spirit" that He wants you to live in poverty. Jesus was talking about being humble in spirit and depending upon God as your total source. In Phil. 4:19, Paul wrote, "God will supply all your needs in accordance with His riches in glory by Christ Jesus."

We are told in Deut. 8:18 that "it is He (God) that gives thee power to get wealth; that He may establish His covenant." The reason for wealth is to further the kingdom; in other words, to do what Jesus told us to do, to take the gospel to every living creature. However, although this should be your main goal, just like any Father wants to see his children do well, God has pleasure in our prosperity. Third John 2 says, "Beloved, I wish above all things that you may prosper and be in health even as your soul prospers." There is nothing wrong with having "things" as long as the "things" don't have you. In other words, "seek first the Kingdom of God" and all the other things will be added. We shouldn't seek after things; we should seek after God, then all the rest will come in abundance.

In Luke 4:18 Jesus said, "I am come to preach the good news to the poor." I doubt that telling the poor to continue in their poverty would have been good news. He came to rekindle their understanding regarding the blessings of Abraham that were theirs and to tell them that they could turn their lives around if they would just take advantage of that blessing.

Jesus said, "I am come that you may have life and that you may have it more abundantly." There can be no abundance in poverty just like there can be no fear in faith. Each is the antithesis of the other. An abundant life is one in which all your needs are met; you are able to supply your family with all their needs and you have an overage that you can deposit as seed into the gospel. You have been promised that as you give it will be given unto you, good measure shaken down and running over; you have been promised that, based on your tithing, God will open the windows of heaven and pour down a blessing you will not be able to contain.

An Abundant Life

An abundant life is also one where you and yours are protected and live in harmony and deal in love. It is a life that says you are a Christian because you are letting your light shine in all that you do and say and you live by the guidelines set out for you in your guide book (the Word of God) and so you are in a position to claim all of the blessings that are part of your redemption package.

One Word on Money

Having money is only part of what is encompassed in the prosperity picture; it is, however, NOT the root of all evil. That scripture has been misquoted. The verse in 1 Tim. 6:10 stipulates that the LOVE of money is the root of all evil. If money is your God, it will destroy you. Look to God as your source and with His plan of prosperity established in your life, you will not need to be concerned about funds. You need to look at money for what it is. It is a bad thing only if you are obsessed with it and live in fear of losing it. If fear continues what you fear will come on you because faith cannot co-exist with fear. Always remember as you start to prosper financially that it is GOD WHO GIVES YOU the power to get wealth; God gave you the money so continue to be a giver! Give into the kingdom, give generously to get the Word of God out to a dying world, and remember you cannot out give God!

God multiplies by division. As you give, what you give is multiplied back to you a hundred-fold. That may not seem logical to you, but it is word based and absolutely spiritually true!

Was Jesus Poor?

Second Corinthians 8:9, speaking of Jesus, Paul said, "He that was rich became poor for our sakes that we might be rich." 'Poor" is a relative term here. In comparison to what was His before He came to earth as a man, Jesus was poor. He took the lesser estate so that we could be rich.

Let's talk for a moment about the rich young man that we are told about in Mark 10:17–25. This young man didn't *have* possessions, the possessions *had* him. Jesus wasn't suggesting to this man that he become a pauper; He wanted him to get his priorities straight and recognize the difference between "possessions" and "treasures" and when his obsession with "things" sent him away sorrowful and Jesus told His disciples that it was hard for a rich man to get into heaven; please note that His disciples were "amazed beyond measure" because the idea of having riches being a stumbling block seemed outrages to them. The entire issue here was not the riches but that their importance to this young man was so out of proportion that it would stand in his way toward any future spiritual growth.

Don't believe for a moment that Jesus was poor or that he asks you to be poor. If this concept is one you have always believed to be true, please, along with the scriptures we have already directed you to, consider the following:

1. Jesus was responsible for twelve men who had given up their sources of income in order to follow Him, and He was their sole support for the life of His ministry.

2. Jesus was fully aware that Judas was stealing from the treasury and yet, with all the theft that was going on, the treasury was still more than enough to keep them going so it had to have held a large surplus of funds.
3. During the last supper, when Jesus told Judas to do what he was going to do quickly, the other disciples wondered what task Jesus had given Judas. Some thought that because Judas had the bag that he'd been told to buy what they needed and some thought that *he was told to give something to the poor* (John 13: 27–29). It is unlikely that they would assume this if it wasn't common practice. A pauper is not able to give to the poor.
4. When Peter told Jesus about the taxes to be paid, He was able to send him to a vast sea with thousands of fish in it and caused one fish to swim to Peter with money in its mouth. No one with this kind of authority over the "fish of the sea" would ever be without means.
5. At one point, Jesus sent out seventy men into the missionary field to teach and heal. He was solely responsible for their financial needs and the word tells us they were taken care of.

Common sense tells us that Jesus was not poor; the blessings of Abraham that were His as well as ours would preclude His being poor and they also preclude you being poor.

As a final word on the subject, let me reiterate that poverty is part of the curse; we are told that we have been redeemed from the curse. The Word says, "My God shall supply all your needs according to his riches in glory by Christ Jesus." With all that the Word has to say on the subject of supply, regarding prosperity in every area of our lives and regarding the blessings that are ours—bought and paid for through Jesus sacrificial death—we should be forever convinced that we have the right to prosper.

God told Abraham that He would bless him so that he could be a blessing!

God is telling you and me that He will bless us so that we can be a blessing!

That is what prosperity is all about folks.

Because Satan has convinced so many Christians that they must remain poor to please God, churches are going out of business. It ought to be blatantly obvious that this is not the way things should be. We are supposed to support the outreach of the gospel and we can't do that if we can't even support ourselves.

Part IV: The "If It Be The Will" Issue

Question:

1. Is it correct to say "if it be thy will" at the end of all prayer? That's what I have always been told.
2. Is there more than one kind of prayer and if so what are the kinds spoken about in the Word of God?

The answer to the first question is "NO" and the answer to the second question is "YES," and I will be happy to list the kinds of prayer and point you to the scriptures that cover each one.

First, let's deal with the use of "if it be thy will" at the end of a prayer. If you have a call on your life and are seeking to know where God would have you go and what area of service He would have you enter, then you would pray the prayer of dedication and would use the term "if it be Thy will." After all, you and the path you personally may be called to walk are not to be found in the Bible. Jesus used the term in His prayer of dedication and commitment in Gethsemane, and if you are dedicating your life and seeking to know the road that God would have you take in his service, then this type of prayer is appropriate and the use of "if it be thy will" is applicable. God's Word is God's will, so using "if it be thy will" really isn't applicable in any other type of prayer. Let me further clarify this area of prayer. Asking for God's will and guidance in an area of need is not the same as ending a prayer with, "if it be thy will." There is nothing wrong with asking for God's will in a given situation if it is not covered in

God's Word. For example, you are facing a major decision in your life that may have you move to another area or change jobs because a better position has been offered you. Saying, "Father, please guide me to the decision you would have me make; and let me know what your will is in this matter." is perfectly acceptable. It is not the same as declaring, "*if* it be thy will" in a situation in which God's Word clearly tells you what His will is. If, for example, you prayed, "If it is your will Father heal so and so" that is wrong usage because the Word of God clearly stipulates that healing is His will.

As I mentioned earlier, there is more than one kind of prayer. Let me give you a list of the different types of prayer, then we will delineate how and when each type is used; and set out the guidelines for each one.

You didn't think prayer had guidelines? It does. Not to be mundane but consider that every type of sport has different rules. You wouldn't apply the rules of football to a game of baseball, or the rules of golf to a game of tennis. They are all termed "sports" but they are all approached differently and the rules which govern them are also different.

The same is true of prayer.

We have the prayer of petition, the prayer of agreement, the prayer of intercession, the prayer of dedication, and the prayer of fellowship. These are specific types of prayer for specific purposes; the final type of prayer mentioned (the prayer of fellowship) is what you might call "on going prayer" in which you are in almost constant conversation with your Lord. There are guidelines for every type of prayer and they are easy to apply.

The Prayer of Petition

This is probably the most commonly used prayer. It is used when you have a need and are approaching the throne of God to make known that need. These are the steps you need to take to enter into petition prayer.

1. Be aware that **God's Word is God's will.** Knowing this, you will need to go to His Word and find out what it says about whatever you are asking for. If it is funds or the salvation of a loved one or healing for yourself or a family member or a home or a car or whatever it is; you will find it in God's Word.
2. Be definite and specific. Lay out exactly what you need. If it is a home describe it—a car, give the make and model, a loved one to be saved, give names, etc.
3. Go before the throne of grace with "Lord, in your Word it says such and such and based on that promise I am asking for such and such."
4. Give thanks for it and know that in the Spirit it is done.
5. Stand in faith without wavering until it manifests.
6. Believe in your heart that it is done and declare it with your mouth and it will eventually come to pass!
7. If you've asked according to God's will for your life, which you've confirmed by the Word of God, then you don't need to ask again for the same thing. First John 5:14 and 15 clearly confirms this. It says, "And this is the confidence that we have in him, that, if we ask anything according to His will (God's Word is His will) He hears us; and if we know that He hears us, whatsoever we ask, we know that we have the petitions that we desired of Him." Knowing this truth from the anointed Word, and then asking again for the same thing is somewhat insulting and indicates that we don't believe this scripture.

The Prayer of Agreement

This is a powerful form of prayer! It is covered by Jesus in Matt. 18:19, which says, "If two of you shall agree on earth as touching anything that they shall ask, it shall be done for them of my Father which is in heaven."

This scripture goes on to say that where two or three are gathered together in His name He is in the midst. How marvelous is that?

When you are facing a major challenge in your life, call several friends who are born-again Christians and ask them to agree with you for whatever you need.

The Prayer of Binding and Loosing

Technically, this is not prayer; however, I'm including it because it is also stated in the same chapter of Matthew in verse 18 and later on Jesus told His disciples that the power to bind and loose in His name constituted the "keys to the kingdom."

You have the authority through the power of Jesus name to bind Satan in his attempts to harm you in any way. Use this God-given authority and it will serve you well.

The Prayer of Intercession

Romans 8:26 and 27 says, "Likewise the Spirit also helps our infirmities; for we do not always know what we should pray for as we ought; but the Spirit itself makes intercession for us with groanings which cannot be uttered . . . And he that searches the hearts knows what is the mind of the Spirit, because he makes intercession for the saints according to the will of God."

The Greek translation of Romans 8:26 is "groanings that cannot be uttered in articulate speech." This type of prayer is accomplished by praying in tongues. Intercession breaks down strongholds. It is a type of prayer that should be used when the situation we are praying about is not one in which we have knowledge of the details. An example would be praying for our nation or praying for the salvation of someone whose situation we know little to nothing about.

Sometimes, if we are sensitive to the leading of the Holy Spirit, we will feel a burden to pray and not even know exactly what we are praying about. The Holy Spirit knows, however, and in these instances, we should pray in the Spirit until we feel a release and know that our prayers have made a difference.

It is a great privilege to intercede and we should be using this type of prayer more than we do.

THE EIGHTH KEY

Prayer of Dedication

We have already covered how the prayer of dedication is to be used. If you are seeking to know what God's will is for you specifically and stand ready to dedicate and commit your life, then you will be praying the prayer of dedication. An example of such a prayer would be, "Father, I'm at your command; I stand ready and willing to go where you want me to go and do what you want me to do; guide me and open the doors to whatever your will is for my life. In Jesus name I pray."

The Prayer of Fellowship

This is the type of prayer that should be on-going. I like to think of it more like a long visit with the Lord; my conversation with Him starts in the early morning (5:00 AM to be exact) and continues off and on all day. He is my constant companion; I discuss my plans with Him. I ask His advice about the seeming mundane decisions that we all make during a typical day. I share with Him how much I love Him and respect and need His presence in my life. By 6:00 AM, I have prepared my breakfast and I eat and then spend about one to one and a half hours in his word. During this time, I ask for His guidance as I read, His wisdom to understand the nuances behind what is being said, and for revelation knowledge that I can use in my life and share with those who may need understanding.

I seek Him for direction in every area of my life; I fellowship with Him as I would a dear and reverenced friend. Jesus has always been my friend even as a child and that will never change. He is my Lord, my brother (I am his joint heir), and my friend. A day without Him would be a sad day indeed. I know that He cares about the smallest issues that I face. I know He understands the challenges that I must meet. I know He wants my highest good and that He takes pleasure in my success.

It is the very best kind of prayer!

TEN KEYS TO FREEDOM

One Major Guideline

Pray to the Father in Jesus' name.

John 16:23 and 24 states, "And in that day (referring to the day we presently live in—under the new covenant) you will ask Me nothing. Verily, Verily, I say to you, whatsoever you shall ask the Father in My name He will give it to you. Prior to this you have asked nothing in my name; ask and you shall receive, that your joy may be full."

In this verse, Jesus is speaking of the manner in which we should pray. He says to ask the Father in His name (in the name of Jesus) and the Father would "***give it to you.***"

Works versus Petition Prayer

In John 14:13 and 14 Jesus is speaking to his disciples about the "works" that they will be empowered to do. He says, "And whatsoever you shall ask (demand or claim) in my name that will I *'do'*." Don't confuse Jesus' instruction in John 16:23 and 24, which refers to petition prayer with His instructions to his disciples (and to us) in John 14:13 and 14, which concerns doing the works that Jesus did and, as he said, "greater works than these shall you do."

The first evidence of the disciples doing the works of Jesus can be found in the third chapter of Acts where Peter used the name of Jesus in telling the man at the beautiful gate to rise and walk. Peter declared to the crowd in verse 16 that it was through faith in the name of Jesus that the man was healed.

When you do the works Jesus is referring to in John 14, you become, in effect, His hands; Jesus will operate through you to accomplish the greater works. The Word tells us in Mark 16:17 and 18 that as believers, certain signs will be evident in our lives. It doesn't say these signs "might" follow but that they "shall" follow. The verse reads, "In my (Jesus) name they shall cast out devils; they shall speak with new tongues;' they shall take up serpents; and if they drink any deadly thing, it shall not hurt them; they shall lay hands on the sick and they shall recover." If a venomous snake bites you, like Paul on the Isle of Melita (Acts 28:5), you will just shake it off in Jesus' name and no harm will come of it; or if you eat or drink something poisonous by mistake, you will come to no harm. You can command sickness to leave in Jesus' name and it must obey. You can tell Satan—in Jesus' name—to take a hike, and he will flee from the authority of that name which has been given to you as a child of God. This is awesome and humbling and powerful. If we could just get a grip on this truth we could change the world.

One Last Word

In ending this chapter, let me say that for many of you the things we have covered may be a reality wake-up call. Go over it again, check out the scripture references, pray earnestly for wisdom in these areas, then let the knowledge of the truth set you free!

YOUR POWER SOURCE

There is a power source available to you.
A power that only you can activate.
It's there for the taking; it belongs to you.
But there are steps you will have to take.

Think of a brand new car on the show room floor
A powerful engine lies beneath its hood.
All that power is there for the taking.
Take advantage of it; you really should.

Get in this brand new car of yours;
A special key has let you in.
This automobile belongs to you
It's all yours; so let's begin.

You turn the engine on and then
You listen to it purr and say,
"It's mine; all its power is in my hands!"
You can't deny its power; there's no way.

You can feel it come alive
As you step upon the gas.
You head for the freeway and then;
Let her take her head at last.

You've activated the power source.
And you should do the same
In your Christian walk you have that source
The precious Holy Spirit is His name.

THE NINTH KEY

Don't Deny the Power

As we venture into this ninth key to freedom, I am reminded of a story told from the pulpit by a minister I think very highly of. In many ways, this story very effectively demonstrates what this chapter is all about. Here's the story as it was told to me:

An old time lumberman had one partner who worked with him in the process of cutting down trees high up in the mountains near their home. They worked together with a huge hand saw, which took two people to wield, and one day, the lumberman's last saw blade broke. He had no choice but to travel down the mountain and visit the local hardware store to purchase more saw blades.

At the store, a young, eager salesman when told what the lumberman wanted said, "Oh my word, sir, I have a far better way for you to cut down your trees." At this juncture, he pulled out a power saw and told the old lumberman that it would cut his work time in half and do three times the volume than his old saw. The lumberman bought the power saw and went back up the mountain with it. A week later, he was back at the hardware store with the saw in hand. He told the salesman, "This is the worst saw I ever used. I never worked so hard in all my life. I want my money back."

"Really!" said the salesman. "Let me take a look and see what the problem is." He proceeded to take the saw, throw the switch, and the roar of the motor filled the store. The lumberman jumped backward! With a shocked expression on his face, he said, "WHAT WAS THAT?"

He had been using the power saw without the power.

That in a nutshell is what many Christians and Churches are doing. They have a "form of Godliness but they have denied the power" (2 Tim. 3:5).

WE NEED TO KNOW!

Hosea 4:6 says, "My people are destroyed for lack of knowledge . . ." In the knowledge of God's Word, we will find what we need to destroy the works of the devil and live in victory.

As Christians on the battlefield of life, we need the weapons that will assure us of winning. We need to understand how we can be more than conquerors in Christ (Rom. 8:37). How can we be overcomers as we face the mountains of adversity that Satan and his gang will create in an effort to destroy our faith? Revelations 12:11 tells us we will overcome by the blood of the lamb and the word of our testimony. Romans 12:21 tells us not to be overcome of evil but to overcome evil with good. Finally, we get greater insight in 1 John 5:4, which tells us that if you have been reborn into the family of God you will overcome the world (Satan's territory) and that the victory that does the overcoming is our faith.

This brings us to our need to understand who we are in Christ and what we have been given as a result of God's love for us, which was manifested through His son Jesus. We need to develop a deeper understanding of who Jesus was and is and how we interrelate with Him in our lives here and now. We need to know who the Holy Spirit is and what is his purpose in our lives as followers of Jesus. We need to know and recognize the gifts that are part of our redemption package, and finally we need to know how to take advantage of these precious gifts and apply them to the business of living victoriously here on earth.

All this may seem like a very big order; however, remember that a journey of a thousand miles begins with the first step and no matter how high the mountain you CAN reach the top, just take one step at a time.

TEN KEYS TO FREEDOM

One Step at a Time

If you have read chapters 1 through 8, you are already a long way up the path of understanding, so let's take step nine and ten so that we can make it all the way to the point of not just believing the truth but "knowing" it without a shadow of doubt. It is really the "knowledge" of the truth that sets us free. The truth alone won't free you until it becomes knowledge within you; until it becomes a part of your very being. Once you "know" the truth, it will become applicable in your life; it will free you to live as God would have you live—free from the curse of sickness, poverty, and confusion; free to live in health, your every need supplied, and having the peace that passes understanding.

Step One

The Holy Spirit is involved in the salvation process. Once you believe in your heart that Jesus Christ is the Son of God, and then declare with your mouth that He was and is the Son of God and that He died for your sake, rose again, and ever sits at the right hand of God, making intercession for you, your spirit is immediately reborn and you are spiritually a brand-new creature. This rebirth process involves the action of the Holy Spirit who will indwell you from that moment on. He has imparted eternal life to your spirit and you have been unalterably reconnected to God almighty.

The process of salvation, however, does not represent the total work of the Holy Spirit. There is an in filling of the Holy Spirit which goes beyond your spiritual rebirth and which is referred to as "receiving," "being baptized in," or "being filled" with the Holy Spirit.

There is a great deal of confusion in this area. Satan does not want you to understand, accept, and use the information that we are about to cover in this chapter. He has caused more dissention in the church over this subject than any other subject I can think of. It is really a tempest in a teapot, and it has managed to bring a great deal of strife to the body of Christ.

Neither God nor I will look down on you because you refuse the added benefits of a closer relationship with the Holy Spirit, but shouldn't you desire all that is offered to us as Christians? In a world rife with evil, don't you feel the need of all the tools you can get your hands on in order to stand in victory, protect yourself and your loved ones, develop a deeper relationship with the Lord, receive a *counselor, intercessor, helper, advocate, strengthener, and standby,* which is what the Holy Spirit would and could become to you? Before you answer that question, please review the rest of this chapter, go through the steps that follow, and then decide if this path is one you want to walk on.

Step Two

Before you decide to develop a relationship with anyone, you usually want to find out all about them. To do this, you get together and share information about each other.

With that in mind, let's explore the identity, background, purpose, and benefits offered by the Holy Spirit.

The Holy Spirit is not an "it"; He is a person—a divine person. In John 14:16 and 17, Jesus is speaking to his disciples and to you and me. He says, "I will pray the Father and He shall give you another Comforter, that *He* may abide with you forever; Even the Spirit of truth; whom the world cannot receive, because it sees *Him* not, neither knows *Him*; but you know *Him*; for *He* dwells with you, and shall be in you." "He" is the third person of the Godhead.

Jesus in speaking to His disciples about having to leave them said in John 16:7, "However, I am telling you nothing but the truth when I say it is profitable (good, expedient, advantageous) for you that I go away. Because if I do not go away, the Comforter (Counselor, Helper, Advocate, Intercessor, Strengthener, Standby) will not come to you (into close fellowship with you); but if I go away, I will send Him to you (to be in close fellowship with you)" (Amp). In other words, Jesus is saying that it was far better that He leave because in leaving them He would be sending them the Holy Spirit. That seems like an incredible statement, but as you begin to know all that the

Holy Spirit offers us you will understand why Jesus made this statement. The Holy Spirit is the implementer—the power source—the field representative if you will. He is Jesus' spiritual persona, in His unlimited form. The Word says that He will guide you and teach you. Jesus said in John 16:13 that the Holy Spirit would bring to our remembrance all that Jesus had taught and that He (the Holy Spirit) would show us things to come. What a precious gift.

Step Three

In this step, we will cover the most common questions asked regarding the baptism of the Holy Spirit.

Question: Does the Word of God support the fact that the baptism of the Holy Spirit is an experience that is subsequent to salvation? In other words, is it an experience that happens after one has received salvation?

Answer: Yes! There is so much proof of this in the word of God that I really don't know where to begin. Let me give you one good example. In the eighth chapter of Acts, we are told that in Samaria, because of Phillip's preaching, the Samarians BELIEVED the gospel and were BAPTIZED (referring to water baptism). Jesus in Mark 16:16 said that whoever BELIEVES and is BAPTIZED shall be saved.

CONCLUSION: The Samarians were saved under Phillip's ministry. According to the criteria set out by Jesus in Mark, these people had been born again and yet they had not been baptized in the Holy Spirit. Although their new birth was a work of the Holy Spirit, it is not called "receiving the Holy Spirit." It is called being "born again."

How do we know the Samarians were saved but had not "received" the Holy Spirit? Because when Peter and John came to Samaria, they laid hands on these new converts and prayed that they might "receive the Holy Spirit for as yet *He was fallen upon none of them*" (Acts 8:14–17).

How do we know that when these newly saved Samarians "received" the Holy Spirit, that they spoke in tongues? In Acts 8:18,

Simon the sorcerer "saw" that when Peter and John laid hands on them, the Holy Spirit was given. He had to have seen some evidence of their experience and considering that the Early Church fathers confirm that they *did* speak with tongues in Samaria and we read in many places in the new testament which tell us that those that were filled with the Holy Spirit spoke with tongues, so there should be no doubt that the evidence of the Samaritan's receiving the Holy Spirit was the fact that they spoke with other tongues.

One other point. This experience is a gift to you from God. Note as you read the above references in Acts that Peter and John didn't ask God to "give" them the Holy Spirit; they prayed that these new Christians would "receive" the Holy Spirit. The gift has been given; whether or not you receive it is up to you.

Question: Does scripture confirm that anyone received the Holy Spirit and spoke with tongues after the advent of the day of Pentecost?

Answer: Yes! Again let me refer you to the book of Acts 10:44–46. Peter at the Lord's instruction went to the house of Cornelius who was a Gentile and preached Christ to him and his household. They were all saved and subsequently received the Holy Spirit and spoke with tongues. It was this evidence of their speaking in tongues that convinced the Jewish brethren that were with Peter that it was God's intent to save and baptize the Gentiles with the Holy Spirit because their experience was the same as the disciples had at Pentecost. This is sometimes called the Gentile Pentecost.

Step Four

The infilling of the Holy Spirit will have a major impact on your life. Paul in 1 Cor. 14:18 said that he "spoke in tongues more than you all" and he also admonished the new Christians at Corinth (and you and me) that doing so would "built you up in your most holy faith"; in other words, it will strengthen you spiritually. Paul was referring to each of us using our personal and private prayer language. He taught on the Gifts of the Spirit but that is an entirely different issue and one we will deal with later in this chapter.

The Holy Spirit didn't just come into being at Pentecost. He has been in existence from the beginning. Jesus said, "Me and my Father are one" and "when you've seen me you've seen the Father" and also "Before Abraham was—I AM!" God the Father, Jesus as the earthly manifestation of God, and the Holy Spirit, all have been with us since the beginning of time itself. The Holy Spirit brings into manifestation every word of God. He was involved in creation, He was the implementer of every one of Jesus' works on earth, and He indwells each of us to empower us to do the works that Jesus did and "even greater works" (John 14:12)

If that boggles your mind, it should! It should bring you to your knees in gratitude for the purpose and plan that God has for your life—for the life of each and every one of His children. He will empower us through the Holy Spirit to bring to pass every truth of the Word of God which we speak in faith. Jesus is the High Priest of our profession (the words we speak); He will honor His Word in our mouth spoken out of the abundance in our heart in love and faith. This is Christ in us our hope of glory.

Step Five

Paul in his first letter to the Thessalonians sets out a formula for right living, for living in peace, for living in victory. He admonishes those at Thessalonica to respect their spiritual leaders, comfort those that need it, be patient with all men, don't render evil for evil, rejoice in the Lord, pray always, give thanks in all things, ***don't quench the Holy Spirit, don't turn from prophesy—just be sure and prove its content,*** hold to that which is good and abstain from the *appearance* of evil. I find it revealing that of the ten things listed, two of them concerned the work of the Holy Spirit.

We need to ask for and accept with gladness the baptism of the precious Holy Spirit. This will open the door for, among other things, the operation of the Gifts of the Spirit through us.

THE NINTH KEY

Your private prayer language is for your benefit, for building you up in faith, and for making it possible to pray about things that you don't have all the details on. The Word tells us that we don't always know what to pray for (Rom. 8:26), but the Holy Spirit does, and will make intercession for us with groanings that can't be uttered. Literally this says, "cannot be uttered in articulate speech."

The best way to clarify in your mind the difference between the **baptism** of the Holy Spirit and the **gifts** is to realize that your private prayer language is **subject to your will** and the gifts of the Spirit are **as the Spirit wills**. In other words, you can use your private prayer language whenever and wherever you desire to do so; the gifts, however, although you must be willing, are subject to the will of the Holy Spirit.

The gifts of the Spirit are clearly set out in 1 Cor. 12:4–11. In studying this passage of scripture, remember that Paul is writing to the Church at Corinth, and he tells them he doesn't want them ignorant regarding these spiritual gifts. In my mind, this speaks to the Church today just as loudly as it spoke to the Church at Corinth in that we are not supposed to be ignorant regarding the gifts of the Holy Spirit any more than the Corinthian Church was.

General Rules Regarding the Gifts of the Spirit

1. The Gifts of the Spirit operate "through" us.
2. They are given for or on behalf of a situation that is for the benefit of others.
3. They operate by the will of the Holy Spirit, *not* by our will.
4. They operate as a work of deliverance being accomplished through us as instruments.
5. They will always uplift, encourage, and comfort.
6. They will never be accusatory.
7. They all operate by love (1 Cor. 13).

The Gifts

Let me give you a quick thumb nail sketch of each Gift of the Spirit—what it does and how and when it should operate.

The gift of wisdom: During the use of this gift, the Holy Spirit will clarify, define, or give a solution to a problem or need.

The gift of knowledge: This gift works in harmony with the gift of wisdom. Your mind may receive the truth of a situation, but the Word of wisdom is often needed to use the Word of knowledge that you've received. When your knowledge of a situation is insufficient, when the facts are hidden from you, a Word of wisdom will help you cope with whatever you are facing.

The gift of faith: I like to think of this gift as "special faith" because it is a deeper form of faith than our day-to-day faith. When the Holy Spirit manifests this faith in you, it will remove all doubt and fill your heart with the kind of supernatural faith in which you know that you know that you know. You can't exercise this kind of faith at will, but if you will become sensitive to the Holy Spirit's leading, it is possible to operate in it as He wills.

The gift of healings: Note that this is a plural gift; it stirs in us a deep compassion for anyone in need of healing in any area of their life—physically, mentally, emotionally, or even financially.

The gift of working of miracles: When in operation, this gift will prove unequivocally the sovereignty of God. God is the source of any miracle accomplished through the exercise of this gift but needs you as an instrument to perform it.

The gift of prophesy: This gift exhibits itself as an inspirational intuition from the Holy Spirit. It is an inspired utterance that comes *through* our mind but not *from* our mind. The purpose of this gift is to edify, exhort and comfort the hearer (1 Cor. 14:3). Someone may be facing a challenge or a decision and needs a word from the Lord that will help them face that challenge or make that decision. It really confirms rather than directs and although at times it may predict, usually it is for a specific person and will need to be confirmed by the recipient. If someone gives you a word from the Lord, be sure you feel a confirmation in your spirit before you accept it.

The gift of the discerning of spirits: This is a manifestation of the Holy Spirit through which a specific spirit can be detected. It is not the gift of discernment; it is an avenue through which the Holy Spirit reveals to us whether a spirit is of God or of Satan. Angels are spirits sent to help us and demons are also spirits sent to destroy us. We need to be able to discern which one we are faced with. This gift may manifest as a word of knowledge, a gift of healing, a word of prophesy, or even through the working of a miracle. It is the Lord himself working through us to reveal to us the kind of spirit we are dealing with.

The gift of tongues: As we have said previously, this is different than your own private prayer language. The baptism of the Holy Spirit is to empower each of us as individuals; the gift of tongues comes as the Holy Spirit wills and is for the benefit of others. It usually manifests on behalf of a group.

The gift of interpretation of tongues: This gift operates with the gift of tongues, is usually limited to three messages in a single meeting, must uplift and encourage, and will never be judgmental or accusatory.

The Ministry Gifts

These gifts are not manifestations of the Holy Spirit; they are people gifted in a specific area of service to the Church. These are the Apostles, Prophets, Evangelists, Pastors, and Teachers through which the body of Christ is to be perfected (Eph. 4:11–13).

God wants His children strengthened in the Word so they can be strong in the Lord and in the power of His might. He wants them edified and built up so that no weapon formed against them can prosper. He wants them properly taught so they will renew their minds, apply the principles of the Word to their own lives, and then pass what they have learned on to others. The Word says Jesus is coming back for a perfect Church without spot or wrinkle. In order to accomplish this, ministry gifts were given to the people of God.

Let me just recap what each area of ministry gift is meant to accomplish:

APOSTLES: Although the person serving in this capacity may not be specifically called an apostle, his leadership will clearly identify him. He is the trail blazer; he establishes the doctrinal guidelines of the church and his anointing equips him to break Satan's claim over the Kingdom of God.

PROPHETS: Many of the gifts of the Spirit will operate through one standing in the office of prophet. Under the Old Covenant they were called seers because by the operation of the Holy Spirit through them they perceived things to come. A prophet will perceive God's guidance and direction and make it known as he is given the unction to do so.

EVANGELISTS: Anyone operating under this gift goes ahead to establish a stronghold; his major thrust is the saving of souls—the calling of men to repentance—as well as reviving of established believers. He's the front runner of many a church which is subsequently established. The evangelist has a vital ministry and without his work others ministries would be less effective.

PASTORS: The shepherd of the flock. He oversees the work of the local church congregation, feeding them the Word of God, driving out any enemy to God's church, and comforting his charges in times of stress. A pastor's work may come after the evangelist who usually strikes and then moves on. The pastor is strong in the Word and powerful in his knowledge of the truths within it. The pastor is known in his community and stands out as a spiritual leader, guardian of the faith, and comforter of those in distress.

TEACHERS: A student of the Word of God, the person operating under the anointing of this gift is capable of presenting the gospel in a way that brings it to life, and makes it understandable and applicable to the business of living a victorious Christian life. The teaching gift is powerful in its influence especially on believers eager and anxious to know the truth of God's Word so they can live according to the principles laid out in it. In order for the body of Christ to grow, there must be anointed teachers to show the way.

You Can Have It All

What I have given you in this chapter is an overview of who the Holy Spirit is and what He does or will do for us in our Christian walk. He operates through the gifts of the Spirit. He is the anointing that powers the ministry gifts. He in fills our spirit when we are baptized and makes possible praying in tongues to build ourselves up spiritually. He will help us to intercede in situations where we do not have all the particulars and therefore, "don't know how to pray as we ought."

On a personal level, the Holy Spirit is our friend, guide, and counselor. If we will become sensitive to his leading, he will help us in times of trouble, warn us in times of danger, guide us in times of decision, and strengthen us in times of stress. The more you develop a relationship with Him, the greater will be His influence in your life. Praying in the spirit daily will greatly increase your sensitivity to the move of the Holy Spirit. Another benefit of daily prayer in the spirit is the control it gives you over your tongue. James indicates that "no man can tame the tongue" and yet doing so is vital to your spiritual growth. It is also essential if you are to adhere to all we have said about the power of words and keeping the Word of God in your mouth. Praying in the spirit is one sure way of taming the tongue.

In rereading this chapter, you can see why I call the Holy Spirit your power source. He is the implementer of your words when spoken in faith and in line with the Word of God. He is vital to your Christian walk and the more of Him you have in your life the more successful you are going to be.

As you can see, the benefits of being baptized in the Holy Spirit are many and the drawbacks nonexistent. The only negative I can see would be if you are going to a Church that does not believe in taking this step; in that event, I would personally find a Church that did. In the long run, however, the decision is yours.

This step will open the door to so many blessings. You will never regret taking it; you will only wonder why you didn't do it sooner.

The process is simple. Ask God to fill you to over flowing with the Holy Spirit, then begin praising and thanking Him for making this precious experience possible. At some point, the Holy Spirit will take over and your prayer language will manifest. If it seems a little awkward at first, don't be concerned; it will get easier with use.

Don't deny the power!

THE LAST KEY

Nine keys
Keys to freedom
From sin and sickness and fear.
Nine keys
Keys that answer
Questions we all hold dear.

Nine keys
Each one fashioned
To help you be all you can be.
Nine keys
Keys to loose you
From bondage and set you free.

Nine keys
Keys to freedom.
With the final key, the die is cast
The tenth key is here:
We've been saving
The very best key for last!

THE TENTH KEY

Develop a Close Relationship with the Lord

"Getting to know you; getting to know all about you. Getting to like you; getting to hope you like me. Putting it my way, but nicely; you are precisely my cup of tea. Getting to know you; getting to feel free and easy; when I am with you getting to know what to say. Haven't you noticed suddenly I'm bright and breezy? Because of all the beautiful and new things I'm learning about you—day by day."

These are the words of a song from the famous musical, "The King and I." I found the words of the song and the title of the play ironic as applied to the path we will take in this chapter.

In Matthew 11:28 and 29 Jesus said, "Come unto me all you that labor and are heavy laden and I will give you rest. Take my yoke upon you and **learn of me** for I am humble and lowly in heart; and you will find rest for your souls." This was an open appeal for us to get to know Him.

I've saved the best Key to Freedom for the last chapter in this book. We will be talking in depth about the process of "getting to know" Jesus Christ—King of Kings, Son of Man, Son of the living God.

Along with these impressive titles, Jesus is also your Lord and Savior. He is your mediator. He is your joint heir. He is your healer. He is your Redeemer, and He is the High Priest of your profession (what you say)!

Above all, Jesus is your dear and treasured friend; He loves you beyond your finite mind's ability to comprehend it and longs to fellowship with you, and to develop a deeper relationship with you. By the end of this final chapter of *Ten Keys to Freedom*, it is my hope and desire that you will want to do just that—that you will begin to understand in your heart just how much you are loved and will reach out and begin a relationship with Jesus. It will enrich your life in every way.

GETTING TO KNOW HIM

In order to develop a close relationship with anyone, it is first and foremost essential to find out all about them—where did they come from, what is their background, what outstanding personality traits do they have, what is their opinion in areas that are important to you, how does their mind work, how will a relationship benefit you both?

In order to deal with all these questions, let's start at the beginning.

WHERE DID IT ALL BEGIN?

When the Jews contended with Jesus regarding his reference to knowing Abraham in John 8:52–58, they said, "You are not yet fifty years old, and have you seen Abraham?" Jesus' reply is powerful, mind-boggling, and insightful. He said quite simply, "Before Abraham was, I Am."

Jesus in His divinity prior to coming to earth as a man was and still is a part of the divine trinity—Father, Son, and Holy Spirit—and as such existed from the beginning of time (Heb. 1:2, John 17:5 and 24). In John 1:1, the "Word" referred to is Jesus. He was there when the Word of almighty God implemented by the Holy Spirit created the heavens and the earth; He watched the downfall of Adam, which affected the entire human race, and He agreed to become the ransom and pay the price for the salvation of mankind. You and I are the ones He agreed to redeem. The price was His life and He paid it gladly.

TEN KEYS TO FREEDOM

THE BIRTH OF JESUS

He laid aside His divinity, was conceived of a virgin by the same powerful creative Word of God that formed the earth, implemented once more by the Holy Spirit (Luke 1:28–35). Jesus became the second Adam (1 Cor. 15:45–47). He lived as a man, walked as a man, operated in the power of the Holy Spirit as a man in the same way you and I can. He was tempted in all things like a man, but was without sin. He called Himself the Son of Man, and He became the perfect Lamb of God sacrificed to ransom back the human race.

Because Jesus was destined to be the perfect Lamb of God He must, of necessity be born of a virgin. Every man born after Adam was born in sin. The bloodline follows the Father so an earthly Father was out of the question. Both life and death flows in our veins but Jesus had no death in Him. On a number of occasions, angry crowds tried to kill Him, but it was not possible to do so. One such attempt was even made in His home town. Jesus said, "No man takes my life" (John 10:17–18) and "The prince of this world comes (Satan) and has nothing in me" (John 14:30). The embryo in Mary's womb was the Word of God quickened and given life by the Holy Spirit. Because of this Jesus' blood was pure and filled only with life; He had the blood of His Father God in His veins. You might ask, "If death was not in Him and no one could take His life, how did they manage to do so at Calvary?" The answer is simple. They didn't take it; He gave it. If you will recall he told Pilate, "You could have no power at all against me except it were given to you from above . . ." (John 19:11).

THE ATTRIBUTES OF JESUS

Jesus in many places in the Gospels said, "I and the Father are one." "If you have seen me you have seen the Father." God took all of His power, His love, His light, and His wisdom and incarnated it in the birth of the man Jesus Christ. This means that as God is love so is Jesus, as God is light so is Jesus and as God is divine wisdom, so is Jesus (John 14:7–10, John 9:35–37, John 1:29).

THE TENTH KEY

In trying to describe Jesus, one would say, "He is an honest, trustworthy, kind, loving, merciful, powerful, dynamic man." Once you have made His acquaintance, you will never be the same; His influence will leave you changed! Once you have hooked your wagon to His star, your life will take on a whole new meaning—one full of hope, love, peace, joy, and blessing; and even though your commitment causes persecution, it will be a small price to pay for the many benefits of your relationship.

JESUS' PURPOSES ON EARTH

Jesus' main purpose on earth was to do the will of His Father God (John 6:38). In accomplishing the plans and purposes of His Father, Jesus set out to save that which was lost (Luke 19:10), destroy the works of the devil (1 John 3:8), fulfill the prophesies of the Old Covenant (Matt. 5:17), do away with and free us from the ritual ceremonies of the law (Rom. 3:20–28 and Rom. 13:8, 9), give us the blessings of Abraham (Gal. 3:13–14), and usher in the righteousness of God in Christ Jesus (Eph. 4:24, Phil. 3:9, and 1 John 2:29) He was our way shower and He became the first born of many brethren (Rom. 8:29). As we have said, Jesus knew no sin but He did "become" sin to save you and me from our sins. His resurrection also involved his "rebirth" and opened the door for the rebirth of each and every born again follower of Christ from that moment on. This is what is meant by "Christ in you the hope of glory" (Col. 1:27). Suddenly Satan was not just dealing with one Jesus but with an entire world of men and women imbued with the very nature of Jesus and able to do what He did and even greater things than He did. Jesus took the authority that Adam had given Satan—stripped him of it—and He gave that authority to you and me so that we could use it to destroy the works of the devil in Jesus' name. That fact alone should make each of us eager to establish a lasting relationship with Jesus Christ.

WHAT'S IN A NAME

One point of clarification I want to make at this point for those of you who may have always thought that Jesus' name was "Jesus

Christ." Actually "Christ" in the original Greek was interpreted from the Hebrew word for "Messiah," which means "the anointed one." So when we say "Jesus Christ," we are really saying "Jesus the anointed or the anointed one." In Matt. 16: 14, 15, and 20, when Jesus asked, "Whom do men say that I am" and finally, "whom do *you* say that I am," Peter answered, "You are ***the** Christ*, the Son of the living God." Later in verse 20, it says that Jesus admonished them to tell no one that He was *Jesus **the** Christ;* note in both cases the use of not "Jesus Christ," but "*Jesus **the** Christ.*"

We also need to firmly establish in our hearts the fact that with His death and resurrection God gave Jesus a *name above every name* (Phil. 2:9).

In Matthew, Jesus speaks to His disciples (and to you and me) and says, "All power is given unto me in heaven and in earth" The word interpreted "power" also means "authority." Then in Mark's telling of Jesus' final minutes on earth, he reveals that Jesus told them (and us) to "go into the entire world and preach the gospel . . ." He also said, "These signs shall follow them that believe; *In my name* they shall cast out devils; they shall speak with new tongues; they shall take up serpents and if they drink any deadly thing it will not hurt them; they shall lay hands on the sick and they shall recover" (Mark 16:15 and 17–18).

What does this say to us about the name of Jesus? It says that He has been given all power and authority, and He has delegated it to us to do the works that He did on earth. What does this say to us about our use of *His name*? It tells us that we have the permission and privilege to *use His* name against anything the devil tries to throw at us; it tells us we are more than conquerors and no weapon formed against us will prosper because of that *acquired authority and power* and our right to use His name—the name of JESUS!

THE LOVE CONNECTION

First John 4:7 and 8 tells us that God is love and if you do not know love, you can't possibly know God. It goes on in that chapter to say that God so loved us that He gave us His only Son to be the propitiation for our sins. Jesus said that when we had seen Him we had seen the Father, so we can say that if God is love, then Jesus is love.

Jesus in John 15:9–13 declared that as the Father (God) has loved Him in the same way He has loved us. Then He admonishes us to keep His commandments and abide in His love just as He had kept His Father's commandments and abided in His love. In verse 13, He says, "Greater love has no man than this; that he lay down his life for his friends." He was speaking to His disciples and to you and me and He called us *friends*.

Love is the final commandment and we have already covered the need to deal in love in an earlier chapter; however, to really understand to what extent Jesus was a living example of love in action, we will need to follow Him through the gospels. Walk with Him in spirit as you read of His compassion toward those who were in need of healing. Watch Him as He reaches out to those who badly needed instruction, who needed comfort, who needed direction. Be there as He feeds the thousands with a few loaves and fishes because of His concern for their well-being. Walk behind Him as He brings a man's little daughter back to life, restores a son to his Mother by interrupting a funeral train, and calls forth Lazarus from the grave and delivers him back to his grieving family. Watch Him as He heals wherever He goes, reaches out to a people who had, for the most part, given up hope of a brighter future, and spreads before them the good news of the gospel. His compassion is evident in everything that He did; it shines in His patience with those plagued with a total lack of understanding of what He was trying to teach them; it evidences itself as He cries over Jerusalem and it culminates at Calvary. This is a man full of the love of God for His creation. This is a man so driven by love for the human race that He makes the final sacrifice and pays the ultimate price to redeem their sin sick souls. Jesus is love incarnate!

The best way to grow in your knowledge of Jesus is to walk through the gospels (Matthew, Mark, Luke, and John) and witness in spirit the man. Get to know who He is—how He thought, how much He wants to see you blessed, and the criteria He sets out for you to live in those blessings.

It is a very different approach to reading the gospels; read with a desire for spiritual insight in your effort to really get to know Jesus and to develop a lasting relationship with Him. This can be the springboard that takes you to the step, which follows.

FELLOWSHIPPING WITH THE LORD

In prior chapters, we spoke of the different kinds of prayer. That information is valid and scriptural; however, in your quest to deepen in your relationship with the Lord we will hone in on the prayer of fellowship.

Webster in defining *fellowship* says, "Fellowship is companionship; friendly association; a mutual sharing of experiences, activities and interests." *Harper's Bible Dictionary* in describing fellowship refers to the Greek word *koinonia*, which means communion on equal terms, a sharing of experiences. Although fellowship as such is not referred to very often in the Old Testament, it is evident that a very real fellowship existed between God and many of the Old Testament patriarchs. Abraham was called the friend of God; Moses spoke with God face-to-face; David had an intimate relationship with God as can easily be seen in the Psalms. In contrast, the New Testament stresses and encourages fellowship with Jesus and the Holy Spirit. This precious gift is part of your redemption package, a priceless part and you should be taking advantage of it!

This is not some deep dark secret that is involved and complicated to figure out and implement. Imagine if you had a dear friend come to visit. You would make them welcome, plan time for private talks so as to catch up on each other's lives, incorporate them into your everyday activities so they would feel wanted, appreciated and welcome. You would share with them your hopes and dreams for the future and would listen to their suggestions regarding how they could be realized because you love and respect this friend and you know they are older and wiser than you and have your best interests at heart.

Out of this time of fellowship would grow a deeper and stronger relationship that would be a blessing to you both.

THE TENTH KEY

That in a nutshell is the prayer of fellowship. That is what you should do to commune with and develop a deeper relationship with Jesus. Out of this will come a sense of closeness, a deeper love for God, a stronger faith in His plan for your life, a sensitivity to the leading of the Holy Spirit, and a sure knowledge that Jesus is your friend as well as your Lord and Savior, that He will never leave or forsake you and that He is the same yesterday, today, and forever. His love is sure and never fails; His love for you is boundless, and His plans for you are for your good, to bless you and to make you a blessing.

You will become more and more aware of His presence in your life, and this will help you to live in accordance with His guidelines so that you can receive all the benefits of your redemption. You will learn to turn over all cares to Him because He cares for you and stress will become a thing of the past. You will learn to deal in love, to forgive as he has forgiven you, and to exhibit the fruit of the Spirit as set out in Gal. 5:22. If you miss it along the way (and we all do), Jesus is right there and it is an easy fix. Just ask Him to forgive you; He will, and that is that. Don't waste any time in guilt; just accept His forgiveness and get on with your life determined to do better next time.

My conversation with Jesus begins when I first get up; we talk off and on throughout the day. I ask Him about anything and everything. I check with Him before I take any action or make any decision that involves me or my family. I ask Him to help me in areas where I am weak and need work; I tell Him I want to be more like Him and ask Him to help me smooth out any rough edges that could prevent me from reaching this goal. I take advantage of all that He offers me. I claim all the blessings that are mine because of Him, and above all, I thank Him for all that He does to help me, to protect me, to guide me, and to correct me.

Live your life this way and you will develop such a deep and lasting relationship with the Lord that you won't be able to imagine life without Him as a part of it.

As you practice this way of life, it will soon become evident that all Jesus' attributes are being reflected in you, and as you reflect Jesus, those that need Him and have never met Him will be drawn to you.

A life lived as a reflection of the Lord Jesus is a testimony that speaks louder than any sermon.

A FINAL WORD

Get to know Jesus; get to know all about Him . . . it will lead you to a level of trust that will become a major key to freedom—freedom from fear, from want, from sickness, and from turmoil. It will also be the key that opens up to you all the blessings God longs to pour into your life.

I started this final chapter with the words to a song; let me end with the words to another. My prayer for you who have read and plan to use the *Ten Keys to Freedom* outlined in this book is summed up in the following words from a song I know you are all familiar with:

"Just a closer walk with thee, precious Jesus let it be; walking daily close to thee; let it be, dear Lord, let it be."

God bless you, every one!

ABOUT THE AUTHOR

Joy Linn is a woman of many talents. She is an ordained minister; a Bible teacher; a playwright, stage director, and author. Joy is also a celebrated poet having won numerous awards in that field. She has been listed in Who's Who in the West and Who's Who International, and for many years was a member of ASCAP. Joy is a gifted and prolific writer with five more books scheduled for publication after the release of "Ten Keys to Freedom." She has written numerous magazine articles, has a book out entitled "I've Been Born Again, Now What?" and has produced and directed several religious plays and musical productions. Joy has been involved in the writing of music for films, and she has co-written a Christian album for children entitled "The Bible Story Lady," which is soon to be released.

Joy and her family are presently living on the West Coast. She is extremely active in her church, has an e-mail poetry club that has reached out to the western states as well as several foreign countries and, of course, she continues to write.

CPSIA information can be obtained
at www.ICGtesting.com
Printed in the USA
FSHW02n1055250718
50884FS